The Burning Tree

THE BURNING TREE

Poems from the First Thousand
Years of Welsh Verse

Selected and translated

by

GWYN WILLIAMS

GREENWOOD PRESS, PUBLISHERS
WESTPORT, CONNECTICUT

Library of Congress Cataloging in Publication Data

Williams, Gwyn, comp. and tr.
  The burning tree.

  Welsh and English.
  Reprint of the 1956 ed. published by Faber and Faber,
London.
  Includes bibliographical references and index.
  1. Welsh poetry--To 1550. 2. Welsh poetry--To
1550--Translations into English. 3. English poetry--
Translations from Welsh. I. Title.
PB2369.W48 1979   891.6'6'11   78-11853
ISBN 0-313-21185-X

First published in mcmlvi

Reprinted with the permission of Mr. Gwyn Williams

Reprinted in 1979 by Greenwood Press, Inc.
51 Riverside Avenue, Westport, CT 06880

Printed in the United States of America

10 9 8 7 6 5 4 3 2 1

For

my daughters

TELERI and LOWRI

in the hope that they may grow up

to read both sides of the book

. . . A tall tree on the river's bank, one half of it burning from root to top, the other half in green leaf.

PEREDUR SON OF EFRAWG

Contents

11

Foreword

I have entitled this book *The Burning Tree* to suggest an outstanding mood of the Welsh poet, the awareness at the same time of contrary seasons and passions, a mood in which the poet brings into one phrase the force of love and war, of summer and winter, of holy sacrament and adulterous love.

Matthew Arnold in his *Study of Celtic Literature* notes a passage from the *Mabinogion* as an instance of what he calls Celtic magic. 'And they saw a tall tree by the side of the river, one half of which was in flames from the root to the top, and the other half was green and in full leaf.' It was enough for Arnold to recognize this as magic, distinguishing it from the radiant, uncomplicated Greek way of handling nature, without prying into the mechanics of the image. Coleridge might have helped him here, for this Celtic tree is a hitherto unapprehended relation of things, an integration of spring and autumn such as Spenser expressed in a more English way and at greater length in the stanza beginning:

> There is continuall Spring, and harvest there
> Continuall, both meeting at one tyme . . .
> *(Faerie Queene* III. xlii)

A similarly startling juxtaposition of the unexpected occurs in Keats's phrase 'fairy lands forlorn', which Arnold also quotes and in which he finds the very same note struck. That 'fairy lands forlorn' gives us one of the best examples in English of *cynghanedd* is accidental here. It is the suddenness and success of this linking of the previously held to be incongruous that makes metaphysical poetry and distinguishes Dafydd ap Gwilym from Chaucer, John Donne from Ben Jonson, Dylan Thomas from W. H. Auden. Out of such a vision too sprang the Old English poem *Seafarer*, which comes closest of all English poems to the mood of old Welsh writing, in which the cuckoo's note is a gloomy warning, as it is in old Welsh poetry, and the beauty of early summer is involved in the danger of death. Up to the end of the thirteenth century in Wales violence could and did alternate normally and closely with love-making,

13

might be inseparably linked with it, and the return of the raiding season of the year made May as much a month of battle and sad remembering as of promise and joy.

Even in the earliest heroic verse this opposition is always to be found, though there is little talk of love. There the contrast is between the happy mead-drinking of the heroes in the prince's hall and the grim death in battle which was being prepared for, the vigorous youth of the warriors and the likelihood of their early killing, an opposition which is summed up in the phrase, 'he paid for his mead.' This payment for mead is in a Northern European tradition, for when in the Old English *Finn Fragment* the men of Hnaef's retinue fight to the last man, they too have paid for their mead. Of another hero of Mynyddawg Mwynfawr's retinue the contrast is made between his shyness and his courage,

> Diffun o flaen bun, medd a dalai.
> Breathless before a girl, he paid for his mead.

So too the whiteness of the skin of the dead warrior goes with the blackness of the raven which perches on his fallen body.

The young men of the *Gododdin*, drinking mead and wine from fine horns and gold, are drinking poison, according to the poet, who was one of their number, for in return for this hospitality they will go to battle and they will probably die. Vigour and death are thus in a normal association, and only the Sick Man of Abercuawg is safe in his deserted hut. The poets themselves often fought before composing accounts of battle and old Welsh law accorded a special reward to the poet who took part in the raid he celebrated. Aneirin may well have been the sole survivor of the commando raid on Catterick, and Taliesin and Myrddin, for I feel sure Myrddin must have existed, were warriors as well as poets. The twelfth-century professional poets Gwalchmai and Cynddelw boast of their reputation as warriors and could hardly have got away in their own time with a bogus claim. The warlike princes Owain Cyfeiliog and Hywel ab Owain Gwynedd were thoroughly trained in the art of versification, and it is Hywel ab Owain, son of the King of Gwynedd, who best achieved this fragmentation of impulses, this equivalent interlacing of the themes of love, landscape, war and death.

The absence of a centred design, of an architectural quality, is not a weakness in old Welsh poetry, but results quite reasonably from a specific view of composition. English and most Western European creative activity has been conditioned by the inheritance from Greece and Rome of the notion of a central point of interest in a poem, a picture or a play, a nodal region to which everything leads and upon which everything depends. The dispersed nature of the thematic splintering of Welsh poetry is not due to a failure to follow this classical convention. Aneirin, Gwalchmai, Cynddelw and Hywel ab Owain were not trying to write poems that would read like Greek temples or even Gothic cathedrals but, rather, like stone circles or the contour-following rings of the forts from which they fought, with hidden ways slipping from one ring to another. More obviously, their writing was like the inter-woven inventions preserved in early Celtic manuscripts and on stone crosses, where what happens in a corner is as important as what happens at the centre, because there often is no centre. That this idea of composition is still potent is demonstrated by the work of two great creative artists of Welsh blood of this present century, David Jones and Dylan Thomas. Of these two, David Jones is the more aware of the antiquity of the tradition in which he creates. *In Parenthesis* and *The Anathemata* are constructed on an inter-weaving pattern much like that of the *Gododdin* or Gwalchmai's *Gorhoffedd*, and one has only to contrast Jones's *Merlin Land*, or almost any other picture of his, with a Bellini or a Picasso to see how the thing works out in painting, how a dimension is created which is unachievable within the classical convention.

Sometimes, as in Meilyr's poem before his death and Gruffudd ab yr Ynad Coch's lament for the last ruler of independent Wales, there is only one theme and one mood is sustained throughout. Here we come closer to the development and climax to which we are accustomed in Western European art forms, but even here there is no logical sequence and the only art upon which one can draw for descriptive analogy, a process of dubious worth, is music of the complex sort. It must be remembered that all this early poetry was written, like music, to be listened to, not read. The hearer could not hold up the poem, as we sometimes do in reading, for the eye to go back over an earlier line. Echoing, running parenthesis, the purposeful re-iteration which has been given the ugly name of incremental repetition, the identity of end and beginning, all these are devices by which the poet attempts a collateral rather than a consecutive presentation of his experience, creating a dimension which thus cheats time, during the space of our listening to his poem. This is the trick which Dylan Thomas brings off in his *Prologue* to the *Collected Poems*, with its returning rhyme scheme, as does James Joyce in his prose experiments. The cuckoo's call echoes through the Abercuawg stanzas, the slim white corpse of Urien Rheged is brought again and again to the mind's eye in the lament for his death, and in *Gereint Filius Erbin* the horses recur with slight differences till one's mind is full of their colour and speed and the blood in which they have trampled and the thunder of their attack, which is like fire on a mountain, until suddenly comes the astonishing line *Pan aned Gereint oedd agored pyrth Nef*, and the simple vowels and simple diction make everything open and clear and calm. You cannot say that *Gereint Filius Erbin* has form or development in the accepted sense and yet it is the assured work of a master in words.

By the fourteenth century raiding and warfare are no longer part of the regular experience or subject matter of the poet. There is still an outlet for the determinedly pugnacious spirit and Iolo Goch's Sir Hywel of the Axe performs prodigies in France on behalf of the English king. But Gruffudd ab Adda's night raid is now not for cattle but for a girl. Dafydd ap Gwilym goes to church to look at the girls and turns his back to the altared God to stare over his plumed hat at the village beauties. The beauty of the world and the glory of God are brought into equally startling juxtaposition when Dafydd hears Mass sung by those traditional birds of love and summer, the thrush and the nightingale.

Aubade and serenade had come into Welsh from Provençal, perhaps through Dafydd ap Gwilym's Norman-French acquaintances at Newcastle Emlyn, but an aubade to a dead girl was something new, and Llywelyn Goch's macabre knocking at the earth-door of his dead Lleucu Llwyd set a new fashion in laments for a dead love. Here again there is a terrible opposition in the irony that runs through the poem.

For Siôn Cent the magic and colour of this world is all illusion and he is the first to take the flattering glove off the egalitarian hand of death in speaking to the great ones of this world, though Iolo Goch in his ploughman poem had already shown the virtue of the simple way of life at a time when the first seeds of democracy were being sown. But Bedo Aeddren, Dafydd Nanmor, Dafydd ab Edmwnd, Tudur Aled, Thomas Prys and a host of others continue to take an unequivocal delight in the loveliness of this world's things and experiences. The keening in Lewis Glyn Cothi's lament for his dead son is touched with the innocence and simplicity of its occasion.

There is not much that is political in the poems selected and translated for this volume. The early heroic work naturally shows a clean detestation of the enemy. From the ninth to the fifteenth century a considerable body of vaticinatory verse was produced as propaganda and encouragement for leaders and their factions in internecine and anti-English wars. Both sides in the Wars of the Roses had their poets in Wales and the prophecies concerning Henry Tudor at least were fulfilled even though the more numerous ones written for his uncle, Jasper Tudor, fell flat. But Henry's conquest of England did not turn out quite as his Welsh supporters had hoped. The absence of political opinion in the work of Dafydd ap Gwilym is significant, for after the loss of Welsh independence the religion of the woods held a positive protest as well as an escape, and Dafydd's feelings are made clear only by the contempt with which he uses the word English. Iolo Goch, chief praiser of Owain Glyndŵr, died before Glyndwr's war against England and he had accepted the situation to the degree of writing a poem in praise of Edward III. We learn what Dafydd ab Edmwnd thought of England and its laws from his poem on the death of Siôn Eos, John Nightingale the harpist, and he regrets that the more reasonable laws of Hywel Dda

B   17

are no longer valid. In the sixteenth century strong feelings were aroused by the cutting down of Welsh woods for charcoal-burning, feelings similar to those evoked to-day by the afforestation or the depopulation for military purposes of Welsh hill country. Lively poems like *Coed Marchan* and *Coed Glyn Cynon* record protests against Elizabethan deforestation.

One of the subtlest pieces of political analysis in Welsh is the first scene of the tragedy of *Troelus a Chresyd*, which was probably written between 1600 and 1610. Like the scene included in this book it has no known source in any other version of this story and, unlike all other versions, it gives us Calchas' reasons for his defection to the Greeks. Apart from Shakespeare's *Coriolanus*, there is no better study in literature of the mind of the Quisling, and there were undoubtedly Welshmen in Elizabethan England who might appear in this light, perhaps even the great Cecil himself. But *Troelus a Chresyd* stands outside the poor, thin, broken tradition of Welsh drama. Its author, so far unidentified, was a scholar familiar with the London theatre and with English literature. A true Renaissance man, like Wyatt, Surrey and Spenser, his purpose was to fill a conspicuous gap in the literature of his country. Hugh Holland is the most likely author, but there is no direct evidence yet to tie him to the play.

Like *Troelus a Chresyd*, William Cynwal's *Defence of Woman* is in a European tradition, that of satirical sex-antagonism, of the *Schole House of Women*, the *Araith Ddychan i'r Gwragedd* and *Les Quinze Joyes de Mariage*, a battle which in France was carried on into the eighteenth century by Perrault, Boileau and Régnard.

Thomas Prys of Plas Iolyn spent years away from Wales, on sea, on the Continent and in Elizabethan London, getting to know its great houses, taverns, brothels and gaols from the inside, as his verse makes clear, without sacrificing any of his Welshness. From English example he may have borrowed the urge to tell a story in verse, a rare thing in a language where prose had always been the medium of continuous narrative. And in his *cywydd To a Pretty Girl* he reflects the London fashion in this matter by abandoning the stock Welsh comparisons for beauty, Indeg, Tegau and Gwenhwyfar, for the classical Venus, Lucrece, Helen, Cressida and Diana.

But it was Prys's outspoken independence of mind and his knowledge and love of the sea that brought in the elements most likely to refresh the stiffening conventions of verse in the strict metres. In all the poems of asking, no one had before asked for and described a Spanish boat, nor had the splendid porpoise before appeared amongst the likely and unlikely creatures called upon by the poets to carry their messages of love and friendship. This is what Sheridan might have called the messenger referential, for no more suitable envoy than a porpoise can be thought of to carry a message to a sailor. Dafydd ap Gwilym was inconsiderate enough to ask a woodcock to be his love-messenger to a girl. Thomas Prys employs a flea for this purpose and surely no creature can get nearer or more secretly to a girl than a flea. There is freshness, boldness and artistry in the work of Thomas Prys.

With the decline of poetry in the strict metres, the end of the sixteenth century saw experiments in the free measures, stanza forms outside the classical twenty-four metres of the highest class of bardic production, and a prosody which did not require the formal use of *cynghanedd*. The new forms were sometimes based on English songs, but more often on old Welsh forms like the *awdl-gywydd* couplet, such forms as had been used for centuries by the lesser, more popular orders of poets in Wales in poems which were not thought worthy of recording, and which have therefore been lost to us, except for the scraps preserved in the folk memory and known as *hen benillion* (old stanzas) or *penillion telyn* (stanzas for the harp).

This book begins with a company of young men going southwards to Catterick to their death in a late sixth-century battle, and ends with a girl washing her lover's shirt under Cardigan Bridge, and a thread of gold runs through from beginning to end, from the gold-embroidered tunics of the British warriors to the golden wash-beetle the girls tells us she uses to drub the dirt. But a thousand years of continuous and copious versification cannot be fully represented in one volume and there are important aspects of Welsh poetry which are not exemplified here. The poem of political prophecy, the poem in praise of God, the nonsense poem, the rabelaisian satire, gnomic verse, the disputation, the *awdl* to the noble patron, the poem of genealogy, there would be no end to the additions and the book would become unmanageable. I have gathered together and attempted to translate poems[1] which I enjoy reading, a good many modes are covered and the three main themes of love, death and the beauty of this world are always present.

The millennium from the year 600 to 1600 saw the development and decline of poetry in the strict Welsh metres and the perfection and classification of the sound-echoing devices known as *cynghanedd*. Technically the peak came with Dafydd ab Edmwnd in the middle of the fifteenth century. The twenty-four measures, already classified in the fourteenth century, were by him tightened up and made more difficult in order to discourage the half-trained practitioner in verse. But a high degree of metrical and phonetic skill is to be observed in the very earliest Welsh verse and one remembers Julius Caesar's statement that the Druids used verse as a pedagogical device. According to pre-Christian Greek travellers to Britain, the word *bardd*, still the Welsh word for a poet, was in use at the beginning of the first century B.C. And when I refer to the decline of poetry in the strict metres with the outburst of verse in the new stanza forms at the end of the sixteenth century, let it not be thought that the twenty-four measures[1] have since fallen into desuetude or become merely musuem pieces. They have been in continuous use, and a knowledge of them is essential to anyone who hopes to win the chair at the National Eisteddfod. And at least two of the old measures, the *englyn* and the *cywydd*, are in regular use by a very large number of writers to-day.

[1] A few are complete versions of poems partially translated for my *Introduction to Welsh Poetry* (Faber & Faber, 1953), a critical and historical account of the period covered by the texts and translations of this present book.

[1] For a full treatment, in Welsh, of Welsh prosody, see *Cerdd Dafod*, Sir John Morris Jones (Oxford University Press). A summary of the twenty-four metres and of the rules of *cynghanedd*, in English, appears in an appendix to my *Introduction to Welsh Poetry*.

Acknowledgments

I wish to express my deep gratitude to the following scholars for permission to use their edited texts and transcriptions:

Sir Ifor Williams: the *Gododdin* selection from *Canu Aneirin*, University of Wales Press;

Eryr Pengwern, *Claf Abercuawg* and *Celein Urien* from *Canu Llywarch Hen*, University of Wales Press;

Lleidr Serch, *Marwnad Lleucu Llwyd*, from *Dafydd ap Gwilym a'i Gyfoeswyr*, Evan Thomas, Bangor;

Y Llafurwr, *Syr Hywel y Fwyall* and *Hud a Lliw y Byd*, from *Cywyddau Iolo Goch ac Eraill*, University of Wales Press;

Professor T. H. Parry-Williams: *Ateb i'r Araith Ddychan i'r Gwragedd*, *Balet Gymraeg*, *Crys y Mab*, from *Canu Rhydd Cynnar*, University of Wales Press;

Dr Thomas Parry: *Offeren y Llwyn*, *Merched Llanbadarn*, *Y Rhugl Groen*, from *Gwaith Dafydd ap Gwilym*, University of Wales Press;

Mrs W. J. Gruffydd for permission to use her husband the late W. J. Gruffydd's, texts of *I Wallt Merch* (Dafydd ab Edmwnd) and *I Ofyn March* (Tudur Aled) from *Y Flodeugerdd Newydd*.

and to

Mr. John Lehmann, who published my translations of Dafydd ap Gwilym's *Woodland Mass* and Iolo Goch's *The Ploughman* in *The London Magazine*.

I am grateful to the University of Wales Press for permission to use material published by it, and to the National Library of Wales for so helpfully and efficiently putting before me the books and manuscripts I needed.

Above all my thanks are due to Professor Idris Foster, of the University of Oxford, whose patience, generosity and scholarship have stood the many trials I have put upon them in the preparation of these texts and translations.

1. Y Gododdin

Gwyr a aeth gatraeth oed fraeth eu llu
glasved eu hancwyn a gwenwyn vu
trychant trwy beiryant en cattau
a gwedy elwch tawelwch vu
ket elwynt e lanneu e benydu
dadyl dieu agheu y eu treidu *(11. 68–74)*

Gwyr a aeth gatraeth gan wawr
dygymyrrws eu hoet eu hanyanawr
med evynt melyn melys maglawr
blwydyn bu llewyn llawer kerdawr
coch eu cledyuawr na phurawr
eu llain; gwyngalch a phedryollt bennawr
rac gosgord mynydawc mwynvawr. *(90–96)*

Gwyr a aeth gatraeth buant enwawc
gwin a med o eur vu eu gwirawt
blwydyn yn erbyn urdyn deuawt
trywyr a thri ugeint a thrychant eur dorchawc
or sawl yt gryssyassant uch gormant wirawt
ny diengis namyn tri o wrhydri fossawt
deu gatki aeron a chenon dayrawt
a minheu om gwaetfreu gwerth vy gwennwawt. *(235–242)*

Bu gwir mal y meud e gatlew
ny deliis meirch neb marchlew
heessit waywawr y glyw
y ar llemenic llwybyr dew
keny vaket am vyrn am borth
dywal y gledyual ynyorth
heessyt onn o bedryollt
y law; y ar veinnyell vygedorth
yt rannei rygu e rywin
yt ladei a llauyn vreith o eithin

1. The Gododdin

The men who went to Catraeth were a speedy band,
fresh mead their sustenance, it became bitterness.
Three hundred were in order embattled,
and after rejoicing there came silence.
Though they went to churches to do penance
death, the tale is true, got them.

The men who went to Catraeth at dawn
had their lives cut short by their spirit.
They drank the sweet snare of yellow mead
and many a musician was gay for a year.
Red their swords; never cleanse their spear-blades;
shields were white, spear-heads four-edged
before Mynyddog Mwynfawr's band.

The men who went to Catraeth were famous,
wine and mead from gold was their drink
for a year according to honoured custom,
three hundred and sixty-three gold-collared men.
Of those who met over flowing drink
only three escaped from the fury of battle,
Aeron's two wardogs and Cynon came back,
and I from my bleeding for my song's sake.

It was true, as Catlew said,
that no one's horses could catch Marchlew.
He hurled spears in battle
from a broad-tracked, leaping horse,
though not bred for burdens at the gate.
His sword-stroke was bold at his post;
he flung ash spears from the square
of his fist, from the back of a slim, steaming horse.
This very dear one shared his copious wine;
he killed with furious, blood-flecked sword.

val pan vel medel ar vreithin
e gwnaei varchlew waet lin. *(300–311)*

Issac anuonawc o barth deheu
tebic mor lliant y deuodeu
   o wyled a llaryed
   a chein yuet med
   men yth glawd e offer
     e bwyth madeu
ny bu hyll dihyll na heu diheu
seinyessyt e gledyf ym penn mameu
mur greit oed moleit ef mab gwydneu. *(318–326)*

Keredic caradwy gynran
keimyat yg cat gouaran
ysgwyt eur crwydyr cadlan
gwaewawr uswyd agkyuan
kledyual dywal diwan
mal gwr catwei wyaluan
kynn kysdud daear kynn affan
a daffar diffynnei e vann
ys deupo kynnwys yg kyman
can drindawt en undawt gyuan.

Pan gryssyei garadawc y gat
mal baed coet trychwn trychyat
tarw bedin en trin gomynyat
ef llithyei wydgwn oe anghat
ys vyn tyst ewein vab eulat
a gwryen a gwynn a gwryat
o gatraeth o gymynat
o vrynn hydwn kynn caffat
gwedy med gloew ar anghat
ny weles vrun e dat.

Gwyr a gryssyassant buant gytneit
hoedyl vyrryon medwon uch med hidleit
gosgord vynydawc enwawc en reit
gwerth eu gwled o ved vu eu heneit
caradawc a madawc pyll ac yeuan

24

As harvesters reap in changing weather
so Marchlew caused the blood to flow.

Issac of the South land was outstanding,
his ceremonies were like the flowing sea,
   gaiety, free-handedness,
   fine mead-drinking.
   Where he dug in his weapon
   he sought no more revenge.
When fierce he was fierce, there was no change of mood,
his sword rang in the heads of mothers;[1]
a wall in battle, Gwyddneu's son is praised.

Ceredig, the loved leader
and passionate champion in war,
the gold-patterned shield of battle:
spears were splintered and broken,
like a grown man he held his place with the spears;
before being pressed down by earth, before agony,
with his weapons he held his place in the rank.
May he be welcomed in Heaven's company
by the Trinity in perfect union.

When Caradawg rushed to battle
like a wild boar, a killer of three chiefs,
the bull of the band, a cutter-down in fighting,
he fed the wolves with his hand.
This is my witness, that Owain ap Eulad
and Gwrien and Gwyn and Gwriad,
from Catraeth, from the killing,
from Hyddwn Hill before it was taken,
after having shining mead in their hands
not one ever saw his father again.

The men who attacked had lived together,
in their brief lives were drunk on distilled mead;
Mynyddawg's army, famed in battle,
their lives paid for their feast of mead.
Caradawg and Madawg, Pyll and Ieuan,

[1] Or, *in the mouths of mothers.*

gwgawn a gwiawn gwynn a chynvan
peredur arueu dur gwawrdur ac aedan
achubyat eng gawr ysgwydawr angkyman
a chet lledessynt wy lladasan
neb y eu tymhyr nyt atcorsan. *(333–362)*

Gwyr a aeth gatraeth yg cat yg gawr
nerth meirch a gwrymseirch ac ysgwydawr
peleidyr ar gychwyn a llym waewawr
a llurugeu claer a chledyuawr
ragorei tyllei trwy vydinawr
kwydei bym pymwnt rac y lavnawr
ruuawn hir ef rodei eur e allawr
a chet a choelvein kein y gerdawr. *(372–379)*

Kywyrein ketwyr kyuaruuant
y gyt en un vryt yt gyrchassant
byrr eu hoedyl hir eu hoet ar eu carant
seith gymeint o loegrwys a ladassant
o gyvryssed gwraged gwyth a wnaethant
llawer mam ae deigyr ar y hamrant. *(668–673)*

O winveith a medweith yd aethant
    e genhyn
llurugogyon; nys gwn lleith lletkynt
kyn llwyded eu lleas dydaruu
rac catraeth oed fraeth eu llu
o osgord vynydawc vawr dru
o drychant namen vn gwr ny dyuu. *(689–694)*

Gwgawn and Gwiawn, Gwyn and Cynvan,
Peredur of steel weapons, Gwawrddur and Aeddan,
attackers in battle, they had their shields broken;
and though they were killed, they killed.
Not one came back to his belongings.

Men went to Catraeth in a band, with a shout,
with the power of horses and trappings and shields,
with shafts held ready and pointed spears,
with gleaming armour and with swords.
He led, he cut through armies,
five fifties fell before his blades:
Rhufawn Hir gave gold to the altar
and a reward and a fair gift to the singer.

These warriors set out and met together,
and all of one mind they attacked.
Short their lives, long the yearning for them by their
   loved ones.
They killed seven times their number of English;
in battle they made widowed women
and many a mother with tears on her eyelids.

From wine and mead-drinking they went from us,
these armed ones: I know death's sad tale.
Before these grew grey their killing happened.
Towards Catreath their band was speedy,
but of Mynyddawg's retinue (o grief!)
of the three hundred one only returned.

2. Gweith Argoed Llwyfein

E bore duw sadwrn kat uawr a uu
or pan dwyre heul hyt pan gynnu
dygrysswys flamdwyn yn petwar llu
godeu a reget y ymdullu
dyuwy o argoet hyt arvynyd
ny cheffynt eiryos hyt yr vn dyd
Atorelwis flamdwyn vawr trebystawt
Adodynt yg gwystlon aynt parawt
ys attebwys Owein dwyrein ffosawt
nyt dodynt nyt ydynt ynt parawt
A cheneu vab Coel bydei kymwyawc
lew kyn astalei o wystyl nebawt
Atorelwis uryen vd yrechwyd
o byd ymgyfaruot am gerenhyd
dyrchafwn eidoed oduch mynyd
Ac am porthwn wyneb oduch emyl
A dyrchafwn peleidyr oduch pen gwyr
A chyrchwn fflamdwyn yny luyd
A lladwn ac ef ae gyweithyd
A rac gweith argoet llwyfein bu llawer kelein
Rudei vrein rac ryfel gwyr
A gwerin a grysswys gan einewyd
armaf[1] y blwydyn nat wy kynnyd
Ac yny vallwyfy hen ym dygyn aghen agheu
ny bydif ym dyrwen na molwyf vryen.

---

[1] The manuscript gives *arinaf*, but Sir Ifor Williams suggests the reading *armaf* (cf. *CLlH* p. 57). Or could it be *arivaf* (I reckon)? cf. *BT* 3 *ny rifafi eillion* and *RBH* 1149.6 *gabriel raphael amriuant ynghymen.*

2. *The Battle of Argoed Llwyfain*

On Saturday morning there was a great battle
from the rising of the sun until it set.
Fflamddwyn's men set out in four bands;
Goddau and Rheged formed their ranks
in Dyfwy, from Argoed to Arfynydd.
They got no warrant for one day's space.
Out called Fflamddwyn, the great noise-maker,
'Have my hostages come? Are they ready?'
Owain, wounder of the east, answered,
'Neither come, nor here, nor are they ready.'
A whelp of Coel's line would be hard put to it
before he gave anyone as a hostage.
Then Urien shouted, the lord of Yrechwydd,
'If there's to be gathering to talk of peace,
let us raise our banners on the mountain
and raise our faces above the shield's edge.
Let us raise spears above men's heads
and fall on Fflamddwyn amongst his hosts
and kill both him and his company!'
   Before the battle of Llwyfain Wood
     many a corpse was made;
the crows grew red before the warriors.
Those who attacked, with their chieftain,
for a year I'll prepare the song of their victory.
When I'm old and decline to death's stubborn need
I'll not be content unless praising Urien.

3. Eryr Pengwern

Eryr Pengwern penngarn llwyt heno
aruchel y atleis
eidic am gic a gereis.

Eryr Pengwern penngarn llwyt heno
aruchel y euan
eidic am gic Kynndylan.

Eryr Pengwern pengarn llwyt heno
aruchel y adaf
eidic am gic a garaf.

Eryr Pengwern pell galwawt heno
ar waet gwyr gwylawt
ry gewlir Trenn tref difawt.

Eryr Pengwern pell gelwit heno
ar waet gwyr gwelit
ry gelwir Trenn tref lethrit.

3. Eagle of Pengwern

Eagle of Pengwern, grey-crested, tonight
    its shriek is high,
      eager for flesh I loved.

Eagle of Pengwern, grey-crested, tonight
    its call is high,
      eager for Cynddylan's flesh.

Eagle of Pengwern, grey-crested, tonight
    its claw is high,
      eager for flesh I love.

Eagle of Pengwern, it called far tonight,
    it kept watch on men's blood;
      Trenn shall be called a luckless town.

Eagle of Pengwern, it calls far tonight,
    it feasts on men's blood;
      Trenn shall be called a shining town.

4. Celain Urien Rheged

Y gelein veinwen a oloir hediw
a dan brid a mein
gwae vy llaw llad tat Owein.

Y gelein vienwen a oloir hediw
ym plith prid a derw
gwae vy llaw llad vyg keuynderw.

Y gelein ueinwenn a oloir hediw
a dan vein a edewit
gwae vy llaw llam rym tynghit.

Y gelein veinwen a oloir hediw
ym plith prid a thywarch
gwae vy llaw llad mab Kynuarch.

Y gelein ueinwenn a oloir hediw
dan weryt ac arwyd
gwae vy llaw llad vy arglwyd.

Y gelein ueinwen a oloir hediw
a dan brid a thywawt
gwae vy llaw llam rym daerawt.

Y gelein veinwenn a oloir hediw
a dan brid a dynat
gwae vy llaw llam rym gallat.

Y gelein veinwen a oloir hediw
a dan brid a mein glas
gwae vy llaw llam rym gallas.

4. The Body of Urien Rheged

The slim white corpse that is buried to-day
    under earth and stones:
  woe to my hand that Owain's father is killed.

The slim white corpse that is buried to-day
    between earth and oak:
  woe to me that my cousin is killed.

The slim white corpse that is buried to-day
    and left under stones:
  woe to my hand the lot that was doomed to me.

The slim white corpse that is buried to-day
    in earth and turf:
  woe to my hand that Cynfarch's son was killed.

The slim white corpse that is buried to-day
    under gravel and a mark:
  woe to my hand that my lord is killed.

The slim white corpse that is buried to-day
    under earth and grit:
  woe to my hand the lot that was thrown to me.

The slim white corpse that is buried to-day
    under earth and nettles:
  woe to my hand the lot that was caused me.

The slim white corpse that is buried to-day
    under earth and blue stones:
  woe to my hand the lot that caught me.

5. Claf Abercuawg

Goreiste ar vrynn a eruyn uym bryt
    a heuyt nym kychwyn:
 byrr vyn teith diffeith vyn tydyn.

Llem awel llwm beuder biw[1]
pan orwisc coet teglyw haf
teryd glaf wyf hediw.

Nyt wyf anhyet milet ny chatwaf
    ny allaf darymret:
 tra vo da gan goc canet.

Coc lauar a gan gan dyd
kyfreu eichyawc yn dolyd Cuawc:
gwell corrawc no chebyd.

Yn Aber Cuawc yt ganant gogeu
    ar gangheu blodeuawc:
 coc lauar canet yrawc.

Yn Aber Cuawc yt ganant gogeu
    ar gangheu blodeuawc:
 gwae glaf ae clyw yn vodawc.

Yn Aber Cuawc cogeu a ganant:
    ys atuant gan vym bryt
 ae kigleu nas clyw heuyt.

Neus endeweis i goc ar eidorwc brenn
    neur laesswys vyg kylchwy:
 etlit a gereis neut mwy.

---

[1]The MS gives *benedyr byw*. This is Sir Ifor Williams' suggestion (v. *CLIH* p. 161).

5. *The Sick Man of Aber Cuawg*

To sit high on a hill is the wish of my heart,
  yet it does not rouse me:
  my journey's short, my little homestead's empty.

The breeze is sharp, cowherds are ragged:
  whilst trees put on the fair colour
  of summer, I am very sick to-day.

I'm not light-footed, I keep no retinue,
  I can't go visiting:
  whilst it pleases the cuckoo, let it sing.

The clamorous cuckoo sings at dawn
  a high song over Cuawg's meadows:
  better a spendthrift than a miser.

At Aber Cuawg cuckoos sing
  on flowering branches:
  clamorous cuckoo, may it sing on.

At Aber Cuawg cuckoos sing
  on flowering branches:
  wretched sick man who hears them all the time!

At Aber Cuawg cuckoos sing:
  bitter it is to my mind
  that one who once heard them hears them no more.

I listened to the cuckoo in the ivy tree:
  my garment is slack,
  my longing is greater for those I loved.

Yn y vann odywch llonn dar
yd endeweis i leis adar:
coc uann cof gan bawp a gar.

Kethlyd kathyl uodawc hiraethawc y llef
teith odef tuth hebawc
coc vreuer yn Aber Cuawc.

High up above the splendid oak
    I heard the voice of birds:
    o loud cuckoo, we remember those we love!

Singer of constant song, with longing in its cry,
    wanderer, with the speed of a hawk,
    the cuckoo calls at Aber Cuawg.

6. Englynion y Beddau

E betev ae gvlich kauad
gvyr ny llesseint in lledrad
Gwen ag Urien ag Uriad.

En Aber Gwenoli y mae bet Pryderi
yny terev tonnev tir:
yg Karrauc bet Gwallauc Hir.

Bet Owein ab Urien im pedryal bid:
dan gverid llan Morvael
in Abererch Riderch Hael.

Piev y bet? Da y cystlun
a wnai ar Loegir lv kigrun
bet Gwen ab Llyuarch Hen hun.

Tri bet tri bodauc in arterchauc brin
ym pant gwinn Gvinionauc,
Mor a Meilir a Madauc.

Pell y vysci ac argut
gueryd Machave ae cut
hirguynion bysset Beidauc Rut.

Piev y bet in llethir y brin?
Lauer nys guir ae gowin;
bet y Coel mab Kinvelin.

Piev y bet pedrival
ae pedwar mein amy tal?
Bet Madauc marchauc dywal.

6. Stanzas of the Graves

The graves that a shower wets,
of men not slain whilst thieving,
Gwên and Urien and Uriad.

At Aber Gwenoli is Pryderi's grave
where the waves pound the land;
Gwallawg Hir's grave is at Carrawg.

In the earth's far corner is Owain ap Urien's grave:
under the gravel of Morfael's ground
at Abererch is Rhydderch Hael.

Whose is this grave? One of good name
who made ordered battle against the English;
this is the grave of Gwên ap Llywarch Hen.

Three graves of three steadfast ones on an outstanding hill
in the fair valley of Gwynionawg—
Mor and Meilir and Madawg.

Hidden far from the turmoil,
the mould of Machavwy hides them,
the long white fingers of red Beidog.

Whose is this grave on the hill's side?
Many do not know and ask:
a grave for Coel, son of Cynfelyn.

Whose is the four-square grave
with the four stones about its head?
The grave of Madawg, savage horseman.

Bet Siaun syberv in hir erw minit
yrug y gverid ae derv
chuerthinauc bradauc[1] chuerv.

Y beddeu yn y morua ys bychan ay haelewy
y mae Sanauc syberw vun y mae Run ryuel afwy
y mae Earrwen verch Hennin y mae Lledin a Llywy.

Pieu yr bed yn y maes mawr?
Balch y law ar y lafnawr
bed Beli ab Benlli Gawr.

---

[1] This is Professor J. Lloyd-Jones' emendation of the *BBC* reading *braucbrid*.

Proud Siawn's grave in the mountain's long acre,
between gravel and oak;
he laughed in bitter, treacherous times.

There are few to lament the graves on the strand;
here is Sanawg, proud girl, here's Rhun, battle-seeker,
here's Carrwen, daughter of Hennin, here are Lledin and Llywy.

Whose is the grave in the great plain?
His hand was proud upon his blades:
the grave of Beli, giant Benlli's son.

7. Gereint Filius Erbin

Rac Gereint gelin kystut
y gueleise meirch can crimrut
a gwidy gaur garv achlut.

Rac Gereint gelin dihad
gueleise meirch crimrut o kad
a guydi gaur garu puyllad.

Rac Gereint gelin ormes
gueleis meirch can eu crees
a guydi gaur garv achles.

En Llogborth y gueleise vitheint
a geloraur mvy no meint
a guir rut rac ruthir Gereint.

En Llogborth y gueleise giminad,
guir i grid a guaed am iad
rac Gereint vaur mab y tad.

En Llogporth gueleise gottoev
a guir ny gilint rac gvaev
ac yved gvin o guydir gloev.

En Llogporth y gueleise arwev guir
a guyar in dinev
a gvydi gaur garv atnev.

En Llogporth y gueleise y Arthur
guir deur kymynint a dur
ameraudur llywiaudir llawur.

En Llogporth y llas y Gereint
guir deur o odir Diwneint
a chin rillethid ve llatysseint.

7. Gereint Son of Erbin

Before Gereint, the enemy's punisher,
I saw white stallions with red shins
and after the war-cry a bitter grave.

Before Gereint, the enemy's depriver,
I saw stallions red-shinned from battle
and after the war-cry a bitter pensiveness.

Before Gereint, scourge of the enemy,
I saw stallions girdled in white
and after the war-cry a bitter covering.

At Llongborth I saw vultures
and more than many a bier
and men red before Gereint's onrush.

At Llongborth I saw slaughter,
men in fear and blood on the head
before Gereint, his father's great son.

At Llongborth I saw spurs
and men who would not flinch from spears
and the drinking of wine from shining glass.

At Llongborth I saw armour
and the blood flowing
and after the war-cry a bitter burying.

At Llongborth I saw Arthur,
where brave men struck down with steel,
an emperor, a director of toil.

At Llongborth Gereint was killed,
and brave men from Devon's lowland;
and before they were killed, they killed.

Oet re rereint dan vortuid Gereint
garhirion graun guenith
rution ruthir eriron blith.

Oet re rereint dan vortuid Gereint
garhirion graun ae bv
rution ruthir eriron dv.

Oet re rereint dan mortuid Gereint
garhirion graun boloch
rution ruthir eriron coch.

Oet re rereint dan mortuid Gereint
garhirion graun wehin
rution ruthir eririon gvin.

Oet re rereint dan vortuid Gereint
garhirion grat hit
turuf goteith ar diffeith mynit.

Oet re rereint dan vortuid Gereint
garhirion graun anchvant
blaur blaen eu raun in ariant.

Oet re rereint dan mortuid Gereint
garhirion graun adaf
rution ruthir eryrion glas.

Oet re rereint dan mortuid Gereint
garhirion graun eu buyd
rution ruthir eririon llvid.

Ban aned Gereint oet agored pirth new
rotei Crist a arched
prid mirein Prydein wogoned.

There were fast horses under Gereint's thigh,
long-shanked, wheat-fed;
they were red, in their rush like milky eagles.

There were fast horses under Gereint's thigh,
long-shanked, grain nourished them;
they were red, their rush like black eagles.

There were fast horses under Gereint's thigh,
long-shanked, devourers of grain;
they were red, their rush like red eagles.

There were fast horses under Gereint's thigh,
long-shanked, emptiers of grain;
they were red, their rush like white eagles.

There were fast horses under Gereint's thigh,
long-shanked, with the stride of a stag,
like the roar of burning on a waste mountain.

There were fast horses under Gereint's thigh,
long-shanked, greedy for grain,
blue-gray, their hair tipped with silver.

There were fast horses under Gereint's thigh,
long-shanked, seizing on grain;
they were red, their rush like grey eagles.

There were fast horses under Gereint's thigh,
long-shanked, grain-fed;
they were red, their rush like brown eagles.

When Gereint was born, Heaven's gates were open,
Christ would grant what was asked:
a fair countenance, the glory of Britain.

8. Marwysgafn

Rex regwm rybyt rwyt y voli
ym arglwyt uchaf archaf weti
Gwledic gwlad oruod goruchel wenrod
gwrda gwna gymod gryghod a mi
adureu aduant cof dyrygoti
erof ac ediuar y digoni
digoneis geryt yg gwyt duw douyt
vy yawn greuyt heb y weini
Gweiniui hagen ym reen ri
kyn bwyf deyerin diuenynhy
Diheu darogant y adaf ae blant
y ry draethyssant y proffwydi
Bod yessu ym mru meir wyry[1]
meir mad ymborthes y beichogi
Beich rygynulleis o bechaud an noueis
Ry dy ergryneis oe gymhelri
Rwyf pobua mor da wrth dy yoli
Ath yolwyf ry purwyf kyn nom poeni
Brenhin holl riet am gwyr nam gomet
am y drugraret om drygioni
keueis y liaws awr eur a phali
gan ureuawl rieu yr eu hoffi
ac wedy dawn awen amgen ynni
Amdlawd uyn tauawd ar vyn tewi
mi veilyr brydyt beryerin y bedyr
porthawr a gymedyr gymhes deithi
pryd y bo kyfnod yn kyuodi
a ssawl y ssy met ar maa ui
As bwyf yn adef yn arhos y llef
y lloc a achef aches wrthi
ac yssi ditrif didreul ebri
ac am y mynwent mynwes heli

[1] The *Hendregadredd* gives *ym mru merthyri*. Professor Idris Foster suggested this as a possible emendation, though, as he pointed out, it produces a rhyme difficulty. For the Biblical background cf. *Isaiah* 7. 14.

8. *Deathbed Poem*

Rex regum, whom it's easy to praise,
I offer a prayer to my Lord above,
the ruling lord of the heavenly circle:
o Good One, make a pact with me!
Frail and vain is my memory of having
angered you; and I am repentant.
I have earned punishment in God's presence,
I have not observed my true religion.
Yet must I needs serve my Lord God
before I'm weakly put in earth.
A true prophecy to Adam and his breed
did the prophets declare,
the abode of Jesus in Mary Virgin,
and the happy Mary bore the child.
I gathered a burden of wild sins
and I was fearless in their tumult.
Lord of all places, how good you are to praise!
I will praise you, that I may cleanse myself before doom.
The King of all lords knows me, won't deny me
his mercy for my wickedness.
I was given plentiful gold and silk
by transient lords for praising them,
but after the lively gift of verse
my wretched tongue is struck with silence.
May I, the poet Meilyr, pilgrim to Peter,
gatekeeper who judges the sum of virtues,
when the time comes for us to arise
who are in the grave, have thy support.
May I be at home awaiting the call
in a fold with the moving sea near it,
a hermitage of perpetual honour
with a bosom of brine about its graves.

ynys veir uirein ynys glan y glein
gwrthrych dadwyrein ys kein yndi
Krist croes darogan am gwyr am gwarchan
rac uffern affan wahan westi
kreawdyr am crewys am kynnwys I
ym plith plwyf gwirin gwerin enlli.

Island of fair Mary, pure island of the pure,
how lovely to await resurrection there!
Christ of the foretold cross knows and will keep me
from pain of hell, that guest-house apart.
The Creator who created me will take me in
to the good parish of Bardsey's people.

9. Dau Englyn

*A gant Cyndelw i gynydion Llywelyn am Madawc am Maredud ac
iw gyrn o achos rodi ido y carw a ladassant yn ymyl ei dy.*

Balch ei fugunawr ban nefawr ei lef
pan ganer cyrn cydawr;
corn Llywelyn llyw lluydfawr
bon ehang blaen hang bloed fawr.

Corn wedi llad corn llawen
corn llugynor Llywelyn
corn gwyd gwr hydr[1] ai can
corn meinell[2] yn ol gellgwn.

[1] The *Myvyrian* gives *gwydr*. Professor J. Lloyd-Jones emends to *gwr hydr*.
[2] The *Myvyrian* gives *rueinell*. v. *CA* p. 153 for this suggested emendation.

9. *Epigram*

Sung by Cynddelw to the huntsmen of Llywelyn son of Madoc, son of Maredudd, and to his horns, for their gift to him of the stag they killed near his house.

Proud its call when its cry is raised,
when horns are blown in concord,
horn of Llywelyn, lord of great hosts,
broad-based, thin-mouthed and loud of blast.

A horn after killing, a happy horn,
horn of Llywelyn's advance guard,
a horn of wood, a brave man sounds it,
a tapering horn in the track of hounds.

10. Gorhoffedd

Moch dwyreawc huan, haf dyfestin,
maws llafar adar, mygr hear hin;
mi ytwyf eur ddetyf, diofyn yn rin,
mi ytwyf llew, rac llu lluch vyg gortin.
Gorwylyeis nos yn achadw fin,
gorloes rydyeu dyfyr dygen ureitin,
gorlas gwellt didrif, dwfyr neud yessin,
gordyar eaws awdyl gynneuin,
gwylein yn gware ar wely lliant,
lleithyryon eu pluawr, pleidyeu etrin.
Pellynnic vyg khof yg kynteuin,
yn ethrip caru Kaerwys vebin.
Pell o Uon uein yduyti, dwythwal werin,
essmwyth yssyt ynn asserw gyfrin.
Yt endeweis eneu yn echlyssur gwir
ar lleueryt gwar gwery ylein,
ac ar lles Ywein, hael hual dilin:
dychysgogan Lloegyr rac uy llain.

Llachar uyg cleteu, lluch yt ardwy glew,
llewychedig eur ar uyg kylchwy;
kyn uu westlawc dyuyr, dyt neud gawy,
cathyl oar adar awdyl ossymwy.
Goruynnhic uym pwyll ym pell amgant hetiw
wrth athreityaw tir tu Efyrnwy.
Gorwyn blaen auall blodeu uagwy,
balch caen coed, bryd pawb parth yd garwy.
Caraf Gaerwys vun venediw deithi,
cas gennyf genthi ny gynhelwy.
Genilles am llif, ked am llatwy; ar eir
y muner nyd mawr ymi vy gofwy.
Gwynn y uyd padiw Duw yd ragwy
rieinged rwych wyry wared lywy.

10. Exultation

Early rises the sun, summer hastens on,
splendid the speech of birds, fine smooth weather;
I am of noble growth, fearless in battle,
I am a lion, my onrush a flash before a host.
I watched all night to keep a border,
ford waters murmured in heavy weather,
the open grassland all green, the water shining,
loud the nightingale's familiar song,
gulls playing on the sea's surface,
their feathers glistening, their ranks turbulent.
My memory travels far in early summer,
because I love a young girl of Caerwys.
You are far from the lively folk of little Anglesey,
carefree under its covering secrecy.
I listened once on a true occasion
to the gentle words of a fawn of a girl,
then to the advantage of generous Owain, my fine fetter:
the English retreat before my sword.

My sword flashes, a lightning to guard the brave,
there is shining gold on my buckler;
streams are impetuous, the day is warm,
birds are tuneful in song, their busy poetry.
My thoughts are proud and in a far place to-day,
going as far as Efyrnwy land.
The apple tree breeds a white cover of bloom,
trees are proudly clad, every mind flies to its love.
I love a Caerwys girl of noble qualities
and hate those who won't stand by her.
Genilles sharpens me, though she kill me. By the word
of my lord, this visit's important to me.
Blessed is he to whom God grants
a bright girl's virgin favour, gentle beauty.

Llachar vyg cletyf, lluch y annwyd yg cad;
llewychedig eur ar uy ysgwyd.
Lliaws am golwch nym gwelsant yr moed;
o rianet Gwent gwylld ym krybwylleid.
Gweleis rac Ywein Eigyl eu hatoed
ac o du Ribyll rebyt yg greid.
Gwalchmei ym gelwir, gelyn y Saesson,
ar lef gwledic Mon gweint ym plymnwyd.
Ac yr bot llywy lliw eiry ar goed,
pan vu aer rac caer kyuoryeis waed.

Gwaedreit uyg cletyf a godrut yg cad;
yg kyuranc a Lloegyr llawr nyd ymgut.
Gweleis o aruod aeruab Gruffut
rialluoet trwch, tebed ossut;
gweith Aber Teiui, terrwyngad Ywein,
gwynndeyrn Prydein, priodawr ut,
gorisymet glyw oe glywed yno,
rac gorwyr Yago gwyar drablut.
Gwalchmei ym gelwir, gal Edwin ac Eigyl,
ac y gynnhwryf llu hud wyf llofrut.
Ac ysymy dystyon am testun ganthut
o essillyt Kynan koelig dadhanut;
ac yr bot am denneirch o du balchure Ureityn
nyd athechaf drin drwy ym gythrut.
Caraf y eos Uei uorehun lut
a golygon hwyr hirwyn y grut.
Caraf eilon mygyr meith arnadut,
eilywed asserw a seirch kystut. . . .

Lluch uyg cletyf, uyg keinyaw ny llwyt;
ny llutyaf ym llaw llat, nys gweyr.
Gweleis angert ri rac kreic Gwytyr,
pan amwyth ut Mon, maws oe dymyr.
Gweleis yn Rutlan ruthyr flam rac Ywein
a chalanet rein a rut uehyr.
Gweleis yn ymo yn amrygyr,
tewi ganllyw a wyr o anystyr;
torred Caer Vyrtin yg gwrtrin gwyr,

My sword flashes, its nature is lightning in battle;
there's shining gold on my shield.
Many praise me who never saw me;
the girls of Gwent speak of me as wild.
I saw before Owain the Angles in their ruin
and near Rhibyll a lord in battle.
I am called Gwalchmai, foe to the Saxons,
at the call of Môn's lord I plunged into battle.
And to win favour of my pretty one, like snow on trees,
when they fought before the fort, I shed blood.

Bloody is my sword and fierce in battle;
in conflict with England a hero doesn't hide.
I saw from the onslaught of the warrior-son of Gruffudd
many thousands maimed, and a broken rout;
Owain's raging battle at Aber Teifi,
blessed king of Britain, possessing lord,
a chieftain declines on hearing him there
with the blood of battle before Iago's great grandson.
I am called Gwalchmai, foe to Edwin and the Angles,
in the tumult of the host I am a killer.
I have my witnesses who have my evidence
of the nature of Cynan, claimant of Coel's line;
and though loins are girded on the proud hill's side of Breiddin,
I'll not avoid battle through any confusion.
I love May's nightingale which hinders morning sleep
and the slow looks of the white-cheeked girl.
I love fine, stag-like horses and well-fed,
the confining of sorrow and arms for battle. . . .

My sword is a flash, it won't do to insult me;
I don't restrain my hand from killing, it's bitter.
I saw the violence of a king before Gwythyr's rock,
when he fought with Môn's sweet-tempered lord.
I saw Rhuddlan a surge of flame before Owain
and stiffened corpses and red spears.
I saw there a busy surrendering,
the silencing of a hundred chiefs through recklessness;
Carmarthen destroyed in a great onslaught,

gortyar y dreis Emreis eryr.
Dychludet teyrnet teyrnged itaw,
gwledic Aberfraw a gwlad Ynyr.
Endeweisy eaws am ryhiraeth yr gwyl,
gweilgig porfor, pwyllad uyuyr;
pell nad hunawc gwenn, gogwn pa hyr.
Pan deurictrawd blawd blaen euellgyr,
bod ewynawc tonn tu Porth Wygyr.
Bid sswyssawc serchawc bannawc breuyr;
breutwydyaw yr bun balchliw aryen dos
ys odidawc nos, neu ym hepkyr. . . .

Dymhunis tonn wyrt wrth Aberfraw,
dychyrch tir tremud, dychlut anaw,
diessic yd gan ednan arnaw.
Argoed nwy asswe asserw yndaw,
eil wytle didrif, didwryf gyuyaw,
adawd ym gwrthrawd gwrthred hotyaw.
Angertawl vy march ymaes Caeaw
ar lles ner Kynan kynwetyawn faw,
arglodic Gwendyd gwynn assy met pawb,
Prydein allwedawr, oll yn eityaw.
Endeweisy eryr ar y ginyaw dyuyn,
dyreith Gwynet gwyar itaw.
Pan amwyth Ywein eur a threui Dinbych,
dyt yn ystrad aessawr dreulyaw,
dybrysseis ynneu yn aroloet y Eigyl.
Dyurydet yn Lloegyr rac llwybyr vy llaw,
derllytid uyn detyf uyn dewissaw
yg Gadellig uro Dyssiliaw.

Dymhunis tonn wyrt wrth Aber Deu,
dychyrch glan glafwyn glwys yfrydeu,
diessic yd gan ednan eneu;
adawd ym gwrthrawd gwrthred gereu.
Adwen gwellt didrif pan dyf dieu,
adwen balch caen coed cadyr y ulodeu,
adwen yueisy vet ae venestri o eur
yn llys Ywein hir hywr dilideu.

56

loud-mouthed for prey the eagle of Emreis.
Let kings bring tribute to him,
lord of Aberffraw and Ynyr's land.
I listened to the nightingale and longed for the shy one,
the spear was deep-hued, my mind wandered far;
the girl is not asleep, I know how far.
When the apple bough end is a mound of bloom,
the wave is foam-topped at Porth Wygyr.
A chieftain is wise, loving and famous:
to dream of a girl proud-hued like frost-flakes
is splendid at night, or may I be spared it. . . .

The green wave by Aberffraw woke me,
it strikes at the land, it bears riches,
bravely the birds sing around it.
There's a pleasant wood with safety in it,
a secluded thicket house, a silent stronghold,
a home for me, easy, hospitable.
My horse is fiery on Caeo field
in the cause of Cynan's lord of glorious qualities,
the famous one of holy Gwynedd, say all,
key-bearer of Britain, owning everything.
I listened to an eagle at his dinner of meat,
Gwynedd came with blood for him.
When Owain seized the gold and the houses of Denbigh,
a day when shields were worn out in the field,
I pounced upon the English wealth.
There was grief in England before my hand's path,
my virtue merited my choosing
as descendant of Cadell in Tysilio's land.

The green wave at Aber Dau woke me,
it strikes at the grey shore with its fair streams,
bravely the birds sing there;
that's the gentle, hospitable place for me.
I know wild grass which confidently grows,
I know the proud tree-covering, its flowers are lovely
I know that I drank mead served to me from gold
in the hall of tall Owain, brave worthy one.

Dym gwallouyed y win oe wenn adaf ut,
yn Aruonic caer ger Hiryell beu.
Derllessid ym llaw llad ym goteu
yg gweith Maes Carnet can ureyreu.
Dy hepkyr alaf elyf donyeu,
dychlud clod Brydein bedrydaneu,
dygwystlir itaw o Din Alclut goglet,
dreic yw yn dyhet, drawen yn deheu.

Aduwyn kynteuin kein hindyt,
araf eriw haf hyfryd dedwyt;
aduwyn dydaw dyuyr, dychwart gwyrt wrth echwyt
Oguanw a Chegin a Chlawedawc drydyt.
Dymhunis tonn mor ymerweryt,
o Aber Menai mynych dyllyt;
dy goglat gwenyc gwynn Gygreawdyr Vynyt,
morua rianet Maelgwn nebyt.
Neu dreitysy tra Lliw Lleudinyawn dreuyt,
neu dremyrth eurawc caer Arderyt.
Ac wrthyf kyuerchyt o deyrnet Prydein
pa vronn heilin haelaf y ssyt,
a minheu ym kyhut heb gewilyt
ef ytoet Ywein hir hywystyl bedyt.
Ac amdawd o wun nenwawl defnyt
a dyfnwys a mi meith gerennyt,
ac ymdaerawd y dreul o dra newyt,
ac amrant hirwrwm a grut hirwlyt;
ac yn llys afneued ym eitunir,
hynoeth oeth dybytaf o dybwyf ryt;
ac os Duw o Nef neu ym kynnyt,
keinuod gan lywy ymy lawr ym hunyt.

His wine was poured to me from the lord's white hand,
in a fort in Arfon near Hiriell's bay.
It was granted to my hand to kill by intent
at Maes Garnedd field a hundred lords.
He pours forth wealth and wealthy gifts;
he carries Britain's praise to earth's four corners,
he gets pledges from Dumbarton in the north,
he's a dragon in war and blessed in the south.

Early summer is pleasant, the weather fine,
the lovely, happy summer gently lingers;
the waters gently gather, the turf laughs by the running water
of Ogwen, Cegin and Clywedog streams.
The sea wave with its great roar woke me,
steadily flowing from Aber Menai;
the white waves pound under the Great Orme,
the seashore of Lord Maelgwn's maidens.
I went over the Lliw to the homesteads of Lothian,
to within sight of the golden fort of Arderydd.
The wave asks me which of Britain's kings
is the most generous of feast-giving breasts,
and it charges me without shame
that he was Owain, for long much-pledged one of Christendom.
Deprived of a girl, the stuff of heaven's light,
who contracted with me a long friendship,
there came to me a new wasting,
with her long brown lashes and long soft cheek;
in a hall of plenty I'll be desired,
tonight I'll be easy if I'm given freedom;
and if God in heaven is on my side,
being with my bright girl will be my lulling.

11. Gorhoffedd

Tonn wenn orewyn a orwlych bet,
gwytua Ruuawn Bebyr, ben teyrnet.
Caraf trachas Lloegyr, lleudir goglet hediw,
ac yn amgant y Lliw lliaws callet.
Caraf am rotes rybuched met,
myn y dyhaet myr meith gywrysset.
Caraf y theilu ae thew anhet yndi
ac wrth uot y ri rwyfaw dyhet.
Caraf y morua ae mynytet
ae chaer ger y choed ae chein diret
a dolyt y dwfyr ae dyfrynnet
ae gwylein gwynnyon ae gwymp wraget.
Caraf y milwyr ae meirch hywet
ae choed ae chedyrn ae chyuannet.
Caraf y meyssyt ae man ueillyon arnaw,
myn yd gauas faw fyryf oruolet.
Caraf y brooet berint hywret
ae difeith mawrueith ae marannet.
Wy a un mab Duw, mawr a ryuet,
mor yw eilon mygyr meint y reuet.
Gwneithum a gwth gweith ardderchet
y rwg glyw Powys a glwys Wynet;
ac yar welw gann, gynnif rysset,
gorpwyf ellygdawd o alltudet.
Ny dalyaf diheu yny del ympleit,
breutwyd ae dyweid a Duw ae met.
Tonn wenn orewyn a orwlych bet.

Tonn wenn orewyn, wychyr wrth dreuyt,
gyfliw ac aryen awr yd gynnyt.
Caraf y morua y Meiryonnyt,
men ym bu ureich wenn yn obennyt.
Caraf yr eaws ar wyryaws wyt
yg kymer deu dyfyr, dyffrynt iolyt.

11. Exultation

A foaming white wave washes over a grave,
the tomb of Rhufawn Pebyr, regal chieftain.
I love to-day what the English hate, the open land of the North,
and the varied growth that borders the Lliw.
I love those who gave me my fill of mead,
where the seas reach in long contention.
I love its household and its strong buildings
and at its lord's wish to go to war.
I love its strand and its mountains,
its castle near the woods and its fine lands,
its water meadows and its valleys,
its white gulls and its lovely women.
I love its soldiers, its trained stallions,
its woods, its brave men and its homes.
I love its fields under the little clover,
where honour was granted a secure joy.
I love its regions, to which valour entitles,
its wide waste lands and its wealth.
O, Son of God, how great a wonder,
how beautiful the buildings, how richly furnished!
With the thrust of a spear I did splendid work
between the host of Powys and lovely Gwynedd.
On a pale white horse, a rash adventure,
may I now win freedom from my exile.
I'll never hold out till my people come;
a dream says so and God wills so.
A foaming white wave washes over a grave.

A white wave, splendid in attack, foams over,
coloured like hoar-frost in the hour of its advance.
I love the sea-coast of Meirionnydd,
where a white arm was my pillow.
I love the nightingale in the wild wood,
where two waters meet in that sweet valley.

Arglwyt nef a llawr, gwawr Gwyndodyt,
mor bell o Geri Gaer Lliwelyt.
Esgynneis ar uelyn o Uaelyenyt
hyd ynhir Reged rwg nos ymy a dyt.
Gorpwyfy kyn bwyf bet butei newyt,
tir Tegygyl, teccaf yn y eluyt.
Ked bwyfy karyadawc kerted Ouyt
gobwylled uy Nuwy uy nihenyt.
Tonn wenn orewyn, wychyr wrth dreuyt.

Kyuarchaf yr dewin Gwertheuin,
gwerthuawr wrth y uod yn urenhin.
Kyssylltu canu kysseuin,
kert uolyant ual y cant Mertin;
yr gwraget ae met uy martrin,
mor hir hwyr wetawc ynt am rin.
pennhaf oll yny gollewin
o byrth Kaer hyd Borth Ysgewin.

Un ywr vun a uyt kysseuin uolyant
        Gwenlliant lliw hafin;
    eil ywr llall or pall pell uy min
    y wrthi y am orthorch eurin.

Gweiruyl dec uy rec uy rin ny geueis,
        ny gauas neb om llin;
    yr uy llat y a llafneu deuuin
    rym gwalaethy gwreic brawduaeth brenhin.

A Gwladus wetus, wyl uebin uab wreic,
        gouyneic y gwerin,
    achenaf ucheneid gyfrin.
    Mi ae mawl a melyn eithin.

Moch gwelwyf am nwyf yn etein y wrthaw
        ac ym llaw uy llain;
    Lleucu glaer uy chwaer yn chwerthin,
    ac ny chwart y gwr hi rac gortin.

Lord of heaven and earth, ruler of Gwynedd,
how far Kerry[1] is from Caer Lliwelydd!
In Maelienydd I mounted on a bay
and rode night and day to Rheged.
May I have, before my grave, a minstrel's gift,
the fairest creature in Tegeingl land.
Though I be a lover of Ovid's way,
may God be mindful of me at my end.
A white wave, splendid in attack, foams over.

I salute the wizard of Gwerthefin,
the most worthy one, because he's a king.
I couple together in my best stanzas
a song of praise like Merlin sang,
my skill in verse to the women who own it,
(how hesitant their virtue makes them!)
the best in all the country west
of Chester gates to Porth Ysgewin.

One is a girl who must be chiefly praised,
    Gwenllian, summer-weather-hued;
    the second is a girl whose denial holds
    my lips from her for a gold collar.

Fair Gweirfyl, my gift, my mystery, whom I never had;
    whom not one of my kin won;
    though I be killed with double-edged blades,
    it grieves me for the wife of a king's foster-brother.

For seemly Gwladus, shy, childish girl-bride,
    beloved of the people,
    I'll compose a secret sigh,
    I'll praise her with the yellow of the gorse.

Early may I see my vigour exiled from beside him,
    my sword in my hand;
    bright Lleucu, my love, laughing;
    her husband won't laugh before the onrush.

[1] *V.* note on page 222 for these place names.

63

Gortin mawr am dawr am daerhawd
a hiraeth y ssywaeth y ssy nawd
am Nest dec, debic afallulawd,
am berw eur, beruet uymhechawd.

Am Enerys wyry ny warawd ym hoen;
*   ny orpo hi diweirdawd;*
* am Hunyt ddefnyt hyd dytbrawd,*
* am Hawis uy newis deuawd.*

Keueisy vun duun diwyrnawd;
keueisy dwy, handid mwy eu molawd;
keueisy deir a phedeir a phawd;
keueis bymp o rei gwymp eu gwyngnawd;
keueisy chwech heb odech pechawd;
gwen glaer uch gwengaer yt ym daerhawd;
keueisy sseith ac ef gweith gordygnawd;
keueisy wyth yn hal pwyth peth or wawd yr geint:
*   ys da deint rac tauawd.*

I am involved in the strife that has come to me
    and longing, alas, is natural,
  for pretty Nest, like apple blossom,
  my golden passion, heart of my sin.

For the virgin Generys there's no end to my pain;
    may she not enjoy her chastity!
  For Hunydd there's matter till Doomsday,
  for Hawis my chosen ritual.

I had a girl of the same mind one day;
I had two, their praise be the greater;
I had three and four and fortune;
I had five, splendid in their white flesh;
I had six who did not retreat from sin;
a bright girl from above the white fort came to me;
I had seven and a grievous time of it;
I had eight, repaying some of the praise I sang;
  teeth are good to keep the tongue quiet!

12. Awdl I

Karaf y amsser haf amssathyr gorwyt;
gorawenus glyw rac glew arglwyt.
Gorewynawc tonn tynhegyl ebrwyt;
gorwisgwys auall arall arwyt.
Gorwenn uy ysgwyd ar uy ysgwyt; y dreis
kereis ny gefeis gefei awyt.
Keciden hirwenn hwyrwan ogwyt,
kyfeiliw gwenn wawr yn awr echwyt,
klaer wanllun wenlletyf wynlliw kywyt.
Wrth gamu brwynen breit na dygwyt
bechanigen wenn wann y gogwyt.
Bychan y mae hyn no dyn degmlwyt,
mabineit lunyeit lawn gweteitrwyt.
Mabdysc oet idi roti yn rwyt;
mabwreic mwy yd feic fenedicrwyt ar wenn
no pharabyl oe phen agymhennrwyt.
Petestric iolyt am byt y eilwyt?
Pa hyd yth yolaf? Saf rac dy sswit.
Adwyf y yn anuedret o ynuydrwyt caru;
nym keryt Iessu y kyfarwyt.

12. Ode I

I love summer time and the thronging of horses;
a war-band is eager before a brave lord.
The wave's topped with foam, there is swift saddling;
the apple-tree has put on another sign.
My shield is bright on my shoulder; by force
I took what I wasn't granted, in spite of desire.
Slowly the tall white hemlock weakly leans,
coloured like bright dawn even at resting time,
shining, frail, fair, pensive, white and gentle.
In stepping over reeds she almost falls,
the pretty darling, weakly leaning.
She's not much older than a ten years old girl,
childish, shapely, full of seemliness.
Her childhood training was to give freely;
as a young woman more lust will fall on the girl
than unseemly words from her mouth.
Shall I, a walking suppliant, have a tryst?
How long must I beg you? Come out to meet me!
I have grown weak in the madness of love;
Jesus, who understands, won't reprove me.

13. Awdl II

Caraf y gaer ualchweith or gyuyllchi
yny bylcha balchlun uy hun yndi.
Enwawc drafferthawc a dreit iddi,
anwar donn lauar leuawr wrthi,
dewissle lywy loew gydteithi.
Glaer gloew y dwyre o du gweilgi
ar wreic a lewych ar eleni.
Ulwyddyn yn ynial Aruon yn Eryri:
ny dirper pebyll ny ffyll pali.
Nep a rwy garwy yn uwy no hi.
Pei chwaerei y but yr barddoni
nebawd nossweith y byddwn nessaf iddi.

13. Ode II

I love a fine-built fort in a crescent of hills,
where a proud form breaks into my sleep.
A notable, resolute man will get through to it,
the savage, vocal wave howls to it,
chosen place of a beauty whose qualities shine.
Bright and shining it rises from the ocean shore
to the woman who shines upon this year.
A year in Snowdonia, in desolate Arfon:
he deserves no pavilion who won't look at silk.
May I love no one more than her!
If she granted her favour in return for my verse,
I would be next to her every night.

14. Awdl III

Asswynwny[1] heddiw varch gloyw liw glas
a threiddyaw arnat geinwlat Gynlas
e hayddu daddyl weith kyn lleith lleas,
gan hun arlludyaw hoen arlludyas.
Ac ym bei arwyd yr yn was etmyc
e lliw oed debyc gwenyc gwynlas.
Hiraythawc vyg kof yg kyweithas;
hoet yrddi ami genti yn gas.
Kyt gwnelwyf ar ddyn urddas o volyant
nym gwna poen rwydyant; bodyant pa dras?
Tonn a gallonn honn; hoet a gauas.
Yr twf mein riein rudeur wanas
nyt ydiw heddiw; nyt hu atas vym porth
yny myn yd oed vym perthynas.
Oi a un mab Duw o deyrnas nef,
kyn addef goddef gway ui nam llas.

[1] H gives Asswsiswny.

14. Ode III

I would beg to-day for a gleaming grey horse
and ride through to the fine land of Cynlas
to seek a talking time, before death takes me;
in sleep to check a liveliness that has hindered me.
My standard as a youth of honour
was her colour, like the blue-white waves.
My memory lingers in her company,
longing for her whilst she hates me.
Though I may do the girl honour by my praise,
suffering doesn't help me; what lineage satisfies?
This heart is broken, it has a yearning;
for the slim-growing girl red gold is no prop
to-day; my support is not enough,
where once was my relationship.
O, God's one Son, of heaven's kingdom,
before dwelling in this pain why wasn't I killed?

15. Awdl IV

Uyn dewisy riein uirein ueindec,
hirwenn yny llen lliw ehoec.
Am dewis synhwyr synhyaw ar wreicyeit
ban dyweid o ureit weteit wouec.
Am dewis gydrann gyhydrec a bun
a bod yn gyurin am rin am rec.
Dewis yw gennyfy hartliw gwanec
y doeth yth gyuoeth dy goeth Gymraec.
Dewis gennyfy di. Beth yw gennytty ui?
Beth a dewi di, dec y gostec?
Dewisseisy vun ual nad atrec gennyf:
yawn yw dewissaw dewistyn tec.

15. Ode IV

My choice, a slim, fair, comely girl,
tall, lovely in her heather-coloured gown.
My chosen knowledge, to look at womanliness
when it quietly utters a seemly thought.
My choice is to share with and be with a girl
privately, with secrets and with gifts.
And it's my choice, fair colour of the foam,
that to your wealth came your fine Welsh.
You are my choice. How do I stand with you?
Why are you silent, my pretty silence?
I've chosen a girl of whom I'll not repent:
it's right to choose a lovely girl of choice.

16. Awdl V

Karafy gaer wennglaer o du gwennylan;
myn yd gar gwyldec gweled gwylan
yd garwny uyned, kenym cared yn rwy.
Ry eitun ouwy y ar veingann
y edrych uy chwaer chwerthin egwan,
y adrawt caru, can doeth ym rann,
y edryt uy lledurydy ae llet ourwy,
y edryt llywy lliw tonn dylann.
Llifyant oe chyuoeth a doeth atann,
lliw eyry llathyr oeruel ar uchel uann.
Rac ual ym cotidy yn llys Ogyruann,
chweris oe hadaw hi, adoed kynrann,
ethiw am eneidy, athwyf yn wann.
Neud athwyf o nwyf yn eil Garwy Hir
y wenn am llutir yn llys Ogyruann.

16. Ode V

I love a bright fort on a shining slope;
where a fair, shy girl loves watching gulls
I'd like to go, though I get no great love.
I long for a journey on a slender white horse
to visit my love of the quiet laughter,
to recite love, since it's come my way,
to restore me from my gloom, and its half light,
to restore to me one skin-coloured like the wave.
A flowing from her domain had come to us,
colour of snow gleaming on a cold height.
Lest I be angered in Ogrfan's hall,
reluctant to leave her, a warrior's death,
she has taken my life away; I am made feeble.
In my desire I am like Garwy Hir
for a girl kept from me in Ogrfan's hall.

17. Awdl VI

Pan vei lawen vrein, pan vrysyei waed,
  pan wyar waryei,
  pan ryuel, pan rudit e thei,
  pan rudlan, pan rudlys losgei,

pan rudam rudflam flemychei hyt nef,
  yn addef ny noddei;
  hawd gwelet goleulosc arnei
  o Gaer Wenn geir emyl Menei.

Treghissyant trydydyd o uei trychanllog
  yn llyghes vordei,
  a deckant kynran ay kilyei
  kyuaryf heb un varyf ar Venei.

17. Ode VI

When crows were happy, when blood gushed,
    when blood was spent,
  when there was war and a redness for houses,
  when the shore was red and the red hall flamed;

when the crimson red flame flamed to heaven
    and a house was no shelter;
  the bright burning of it was easily seen
  from the White Fort near Menai's shore.

On the third day of May, three hundred ships foundered
    of the fleet of the king's household,
  and a beardless warrior put to flight
  a thousand leaders on Menai water.

18. Awdl VII

Pann[1] ucher uchet, pann achupet freinc,
 pann ffaraon foet,
 pann vu yryf am gyryf am galet,
 pann vei aryf am varyf a vyryet;

yng goet Gorwynwy yng gordibet Lloegyr
 a llygru y threfet,
 llaw ar groes, llu a dygrysset;

a llad a lliwet a gwaetlet y levyn
 a gwaetliw ar giwet
 a gwaetlen am benn a bannet
 a gwaetlan a grann yn greulet.

[1] *H* gives *Pum* here, but this does not make sense. *Pann* is clearly the word intended.

18. Ode VII

When the sky darkened above, when foreigners were taken,
    when the king was routed,
  when warriors were armed for battle,
  when there was a weapon struck at a beard;

in Gorwynwy woods punishing England
    and spoiling its homesteads;
  with a hand on the cross a host rushed forward.

There was killing, and a band with blood-sprinkled blades,
    and the colour of blood on a rabble;
  a bloody sheet over heads and leaders,
  a place of blood and blood-stained cheeks.

19. Marwnad Llywelyn ap Gruffudd

Oer gallon dan vron o vraw allwynin
  am vrenhin derwin dor Aberffraw.
Eur dilyf yn a delit oe law,
  eur daleith oed deilwng idaw.
Eurgyrn eur deyrn nym daw llewenyd
  Llywelyn, nyt ryd ym rwyd wisgaw.
Gwae vi am arglwyd, gwalch di waratwyd,
  gwae vi or aflwyd y dramgwydaw.
Gwae vi or gollet, gwae vi or dynghet,
  gwae vi or clywet vot clwyf arnaw.
Gwersyll Katwaladyr, gwaessaf llif daradyr,
  gwas rud y baladyr, balawc eur llaw,
gwascarawd alaf, gwiscawd bop gaeaf
  gwisgoed ymdanaf y ymdanaw.
Bucheslaw arglwyd, nyn llwyd yn llaw;
buched dragywyd a dric idaw.
Ys meu lit wrth Seis am vyn treisiaw;
ys meu rac angeu angen gwynaw;
ys meu gan deunyd ymdiuanw a Duw
  am edewis hebddaw.
Ys meu ganmawl heb dawl, heb daw,
ys meu vyth bellach y veith bwyllaw.
Ys meu ym dynoedyl amdanaw alar;
  canys meu alar ys meu wylaw.
Arglwyd a golleis, gallaf hir vraw;
arglwyd teyrnblas a las o law.
Arglwyd kywir gwyr gwarandaw arnaf
  uchet y kwynaf: och or kwynaw!
Arglwyd llwyd kyn llad y deunaw,
arglwyd llary neut llawr y ystaw.
Arglwyd glew val llew yn llywyaw eluyd,
  arglwyd aflonyd y aflunyaw.
Arglwyd kanatlwyd kynn adaw ewreis
  ny lyfassei Seis y ogleissyaw.

19. The Death of Llywelyn ap Gruffudd

The heart is cold under a breast of pitiful fear
   for a king, the oaken door of Aberffraw.
Fine gold was paid to us from his hand
and he deserved the golden chaplet.
Golden horns of a golden king do not bring me the joy
   of Llywelyn; I am not free to arm as I would.
Woe to me for my lord, the unshamed hawk,
   woe for the calamity of his bringing down.
Woe for the loss, woe for the destiny,
   woe for the news that he has a wound.
Cadwaladr of defence, protection's sharp piercer,
   he of the red spear, golden-handed ruler,
he shared out wealth, every winter he dressed me
   in the garments he had worn.
Lord of great herds, there's no more prospering,
but for him there remains eternal life.
My wrath's on the Englishman for despoiling me;
mine is it now to bewail death's need.
I have cause to speak harshly with God
   who has left me without him.
Mine is it to praise without stint or stop,
mine is it from now on long to remember him.
All my life long my grief will be for him;
   since the grief is mine, mine is the weeping.
I've lost a lord and I grasp a long fear,
for a hand has killed the lord of the court.
O good true Lord, listen to me,
   how loud I bewail; woe to the wailing!
Lord of armies before the killing of the eighteen,
liberal lord, lone hero ordering battle,
brave lord, like a lion directing the world,
   a lord always restless to destroy,
lord of lucky ventures, before leaving his splendour;
   no Englishmen would dare to wound him.

F   81

Arglwyd neut maendo man daw Kymry,
  or llin a dyly daly Aberffraw.
Arglwyd Grist mor wyf drist drostaw!
Arglwyd gwir gwaret y ganthaw.
O gledyfawt trwm tramgwyd arnaw,
o gledyfeu hir yn y diriaw,
o glwyd am vy rwyf yssy mrwyfaw,
o glywet lludet llyw Bodvaeaw.
Kwbyl o was a las o law ysgereint,
  kwbyl vreint y hyneint oed ohonaw;
kannwyll teyrned, kadarnllew Gwyned,
  kadeir anryded reit oed wrthaw.
O leith Prydein veith, kwynlleith kanllaw,
o lad llew Nancoel, lluryc Nancaw.
Llawer deigyr hylithry yn hwylaw ar rud,
  llawer ystlys rud a rwyc arnaw;
llawer gwaet am draet wedy ymdreidyaw,
llawer gwedw a gwaed y amdanaw,
llawer medwl trwm yn tonnwyaw,
llawer mab heb dat gwedy y adaw,
llawer hendref vreith gwedy llwybyr godeith
  a llawer diffeith drwy anreith draw;
llawer llef druan ual ban vu Gamlan,
  llawer deigyr dros rann gwedyr greinyaw.
O leas gwanas gwanar eurllaw,
o leith Llywelyn cof dyn nym daw.
Oeruelawc callon dan vronn o vraw,
rewyd val crinwyd yssyn crinaw.
Pony welwch chwi hynt y gwynt ar glaw?
Pony welwch chwi r deri yn ymdaraw?
Pony welwch chwi r mor yn merwinaw yr tir?
  Pony welwch chwi r gwir yn ymgyweiraw?
Pony welwch chwi r heul yn hwylaw r awyr?
  Pony welwch chwi r syr wedyr syrthiaw?
Pany chredwch chwi y Duw, dynyadon ynvyt?
  Pany welwch chwi r byt wedyr bydyaw?
Och hyt attat ti Duw na daw mor tros dir!
  Pa beth yn gedir y ohiriaw?
Nyt oes le y kyrcher rac carchar braw,

A lord who was roofstone where the Welsh gather,
   of the line which should hold sway in Aberffraw.
Lord Christ, how grieved I am for him!
O true Lord, release me with him.
His fall came from the heavy sword-stroke,
from the long swords crushing him down.
By the wound on my king I am dismayed
and the news of the weariness of Bodfaeo's lord.
A complete man was killed by a hostile hand;
   every privilege of old age sprang from him,
candle of kingship, strong lion of Gwynedd,
   chair of honour; there was need of him.
For the death of all Britain, a deathsong for the leader,
for the killing of Nancoel's lion, of Nancaw's shield.
Many a sliding tear runs down the cheek,
   many a flank is red and torn,
much blood has soaked about the feet,
many a widow shrieks for him,
many a sad mind now breaks down,
many a son's left fatherless,
many a homestead stained in the fire's path
   and many a wilderness left by the plunderer,
many a piteous cry, as once at Camlan,
many a tear has fallen down the cheek!
For the killing of our prop, our golden-handed king,
for Llywelyn's death, I remember no one.
The heart is chilled under a breast of fear,
lust shrivels like dry branches.
See you not the way of the wind and the rain?
See you not the oaks beat together?
See you not the sea stinging the land?
   See you not the truth equipping?
See you not the sun sailing the sky?
   See you not the stars have fallen?
Do you not believe God, demented men?
   See you not the end of existence?
A sigh to you, God, that the sea may come over the land!
   Why are we left to linger?
There's no retreat from the prison of fear,

nyt oes le y trigyer: och or trigyaw!
Nyt oes na chyngor, na chlo nac egor
    unfford y escor brwyn gyngor braw.
Pob teulu teilwng oed idaw,
pob kedwyr kedwynt adanaw.
Pob dengyn a dyngynt oe law,
pob gwledic, pob gwlat oed eidaw.
Pob cantref, pob tref ynt yn treidyaw,
pob tylwyth, pob llwyth yssyn llithraw.
Pob gwann, pob kadarn kadwet oe law,
pob mab yn y grut yssyn udaw.
Bychan lles oed ym am vyn twyllaw,
gadel penn arnaf heb penn arnaw.
Penn pan las ny bu gas gymraw,
penn pan las oed lessach peidyaw;
penn milwr, penn molyant rac llaw,
penn dragon, penn dreic oed arnaw;
penn Llywelyn dec dygyn a vraw byt
    bot pawl haearn trwydaw;
penn varglwyd, poen dygyngwyd am daw,
penn veneit heb vanac arnaw;
penn a vu berchen ar barch naw canwlat
    a naw canwled idaw;
penn teyrn, heyrn heeit oe law,
penn teyrn, walch balch bwlch y deifnaw;
penn teyrneid vleid vlaengar ganthaw,
penn teyrnef, nef y nawd arnaw!
Gwyndeyrn orthyrn wrthaw gwendoryf
gorof gorvynt hynt hyt Lydaw.
Gwir vreinyawl vrenhin Aberffraw,
gwenwlat nef boet adef idaw!

there's nowhere to dwell, alas for the dwelling!
There is no counsel, no lock, no opening,
    no way of delivery from terror's sad counsel.
Each retinue was worthy of him
and every warrior stayed about him,
every dogged one swore by his hand,
every ruler, every province was his;
every district, every homestead's unsettled,
every clan and line now falls.
The weak and strong were kept by his hand,
every child now weeps in his cradle.
Little good it did me to be tricked
into leaving my head on, with no head on him.
A head which, falling, made panic welcome;
a head which, falling, made it better to give up;
a soldier's head, a head for praise henceforth;
a leader's head, a dragon's head was on him,
head of fair, dogged Llywelyn; it shocks the world
    that an iron stake should pierce it.
My lord's head, a harsh-falling pain is mine,
my soul's head, which has no memorial;
a head which owned honour in nine hundred lands,
    with the homage of nine hundred feasts;
a king's head, iron flew from his hand;
a king's head, a proud hawk breaching a gap;
a regal head of a thrusting wolf,
a king's head this; may Heaven be its refuge!
A magnificent lord, a blessed host with him;
proud sustainer of the Breton voyage.[1]
True regal king of Aberffraw,
may Heaven's white kingdom be his abode!

[1] I cannot pretend to be sure of the meaning of these two lines.

20. Lleidr Serch

Euthum wythwaith, glwyfiaith glau,
i'r wig hwnt, orwag hyntiau;
bûm fal gwr angall allan
yn gwylio tŷ heb gael tân.
Hawdd gennyf, hoywdda gynnydd,
myn gwir Dduw, cyn no gwawr ddydd,
er mwyn Gwen yn ddiennig
encil i wegil y wig.
Gwawr y wig sy i'm digiaw,
gŵr ar draed i garu draw;
diobaith wyf, 'rwyf rewin
o haul y wig, heiliai win.
O dai o'm gŵyl rhai yn rhedeg
yn ardal boen dâl bun deg,
wyf yno, rhyfelglo rhwyd,
carnlleidr, medd mab aillt cernllwyd.
Nid wyf leidr ar daflawdrwydd
yn gochlyd tywyn-bryd dydd:
lleidr wyf, mae clwyf i'm clymu,
lleidr merch deg, nid lleidr march du;
nid lleidr myharen heno,
lleidr meinwen drwy ddien dro;
nid lleidr buarth gwartheg,
lleidr hon, wedd ton, dan wŷdd teg;
lleidr eres hudoles hy,
lleidr poendaith, nid lleidr pandy;
lleidr dirwyn morwyn nid mau,
lleidr purserch, nid lleidr pyrsau;
nid wyf leidr un llwdn carnawl,
arnaf ni bu hwyaf hawl:
lledrad gariad a'm gorwyf;
lleidryn, boen efyn, bun wyf.

20. *Thief of Love*

Eight times I've gone (quick-wounding words)
to yonder woods on fruitless errands;
I was a madman out of doors,
house-keeping without finding fire.
By God, I find it easy
(may it succeed!) before dawn comes
to retreat to the wood's far side,
eagerly, for the sake of a girl.
Dawn in the woods is a plague
to a man walking to a far love.
I am desperate, I am ruined
by the sun of the woods, which once poured wine.
If from houses they see me running
in the pain-paying region of the fair girl,
I'm there, in a fighting net,
an arrant thief, says the grey-cheeked churl.
But I'm no stable-loft thief,
avoiding day's bright face.
I am a thief, a wound binds me,
thief of a fair girl, not a black stallion;
for tonight no thief of a ram,
thief of a maiden this happy time;
no thief of a cattle enclosure,
thief of her, wave-coloured, in the fair wood;
thief of a strange, bold enchantress,
not of a fulling mill, but a foul journey;
agonised thief of a girl who's not mine,
thief of pure love, no thief of purses;
no thief of a young hoofed beast,
yet never was a claim so far-reaching upon me.
Stolen love now overcomes me;
shackle of pain, I am the thief of a girl.

21. Offeren y Llwyn

Lle digrif y bûm heddiw
dan fentyll y gwyrddgyll gwiw
yn gwarando ddechrau dydd
y ceiliog bronfraith celfydd
yn canu englyn alathr,
arwyddion a llithion llathr.
Pellennig, pwyll ei annwyd,
pell ei siwrnai'r llatai llwyd.
Yma y doeth o swydd goeth Gaer
am ei erchi o'm eurchwaer,
geiriog, heb un gair gwarant,
sef y cyrch i nentyrch nant.
Morfudd a'i hanfonasai,
mydr ganiadaeth mab maeth Mai.
Amdano yr oedd gasmai
o flodau mwyn gangau Mai,
a'i gasul, debygesynt,
o esgyll, gwyrdd fentyll, gwynt.
Nid oedd yna, myn Duw mawr,
ond aur oll yn do'r allawr.
Mi a glywwn mewn gloywiaith
ddatganu, nid methu, maith,
darllain i'r plwyf, nid rhwyf rhus,
efengyl yn ddifyngus.
Codi ar fryn ynn yna
afrlladen o ddeilen dda.
Ac eos gain fain fangaw
o gwr y llwyn gar ei llaw,
clerwraig nant, i gant a gân
cloch aberth, clau ei chwiban,
a dyrchafel yr aberth
hyd y nen uwchben y berth;
a chrefydd i'n Dofydd Dad
a charegl nwyf a chariad.

21. The Woodland Mass

A pleasant place I was at to-day,
under mantles of the worthy green hazel,
listening at day's beginning
to the skilful cock thrush
singing a splendid stanza
of fluent signs and symbols;
a stranger here, wisdom his nature,
a brown messenger who had journeyed far,
coming from rich Carmarthenshire
at my golden girl's command.
Wordy, yet with no password,
he comes to the sky of this valley.
It was Morfudd who sent it,
this metrical singing of May's foster son.
About him was a setting
of flowers of the sweet boughs of May,
like green mantles, his chasuble
was of the wings of the wind.
There was here, by the great God,
nothing but gold in the altar's canopy.
I heard, in polished language,
a long and faultless chanting,
an unhesitant reading to the people
of a gospel without mumbling;
the elevation, on the hill of ash trees,
of the holy wafer from the good leaf.
Then the slim eloquent nightingale
from the corner of a grove nearby,
poetess of the valley, sings to the many
the Sanctus bell in lively whistling.
The sacrifice is raised
up to the sky above the bush,
devotion to God the Father,
the chalice of ecstasy and love.

Bodlon wyf i'r ganiadaeth,
bedwlwyn o'r coed mwyn a'i maeth.

The psalmody contents me;
it was bred of a birch-grove in the sweet woods.

22. Merched Llanbadarn

Plygu rhag llid yr ydwyf,
pla ar holl ferched y plwyf!
Am na chefais, drais drawsoed,
onaddun yr un erioed,
na morwyn, fwyn ofynaig,
na merch fach, na gwrach, na gwraig.
Py rusiant, py ddireidi,
py fethiant, na fynnant fi?
Py ddrwg i riain feinael
yng nghoed tywylldew fy nghael?
Nid oedd gywilydd iddi
yng ngwâl dail fy ngweled i.
Ni bu amser na charwn
(ni bu mor lud hud â hwn,
anad gwŷr annwyd Garwy)
yn y dydd ai un ai dwy.
Ac er hynny nid oedd nes
ym gael un no'm gelynes.
Ni bu Sul yn Llanbadarn
na bewn, ac eraill a'i barn,
â'm wyneb at y ferch goeth
a'm gwegil at Dduw gwiwgoeth.
A gwedy'r hir edrychwyf
dros fy mhlu ar draws fy mhlwyf,
y dywaid un fun fygrgroyw
wrth y llall hylwyddgall hoyw,
'Y mab llwyd wyneb mursen
a gwallt ei chwaer ar ei ben,
godinabus fydd golwg
gŵyr ei ddrem; da y gŵyr ddrwg.'
'Ai'n rhith hynny yw ganthaw?'
yw gair y llall gar ei llaw;
'Ateb ni chaiff tra fo fyd;
wtied i ddiawl, beth ynfyd!'

22. *The Girls of Llanbadarn*

I bow before this passion;
a plague on the parish girls!
Because, o force of longing,
I've never had one of them!
No sweet and hoped for maiden,
nor young girl, nor hag, nor wife.
What recoiling, what malice,
what lack makes them not want me?
What harm to a fine-browed girl
to have me in the thick dark wood?
It were no shame for her
to see me in a lair of leaves.
No one's been so bewitched
save the men of Garwy's nature,
for no day do I fall in love
with fewer than one or two,
yet no nearer to having one
than if she were my foe.
Each Sunday at Llanbadarn
I've stood, let others witness,
with my face towards the fine girl
and my back to the pure God.
And after my long staring
over my plumed hat and over the people,
one girl says, piercingly clear,
to the other, who's quick to see it,
'The pale fellow with the affected look
and his sister's hair on his head,
adulterously he glances,
this crooked looker versed in wickedness.'
'Do you think he's pretending?'
says the other girl at her side.
'He'll never get an answer;
let the fool get out to the Devil!'

Talmithr ym reg y loywferch,
tâl bychan am syfrdan serch.
Rhaid oedd ym fedru peidiaw
â'r foes hon, breuddwydion braw.
Ys dir ym fyned fal gŵr
yn feudwy, swydd anfadwr.
O dra disgwyl, dysgiad certh,
drach 'y nghefn, drych anghyfnerth,
neur dderyw ym, gerddrym gâr,
bengamu heb un gymar.

The bright girl's gift amazes me,
small payment for one dazed with love;
and it's made me abandon
these ways, these visions of terror.
I'd best become a hermit,
or live like a law-breaker.
O strange lesson, through too much looking
over my shoulder, a picture of weakness
I've had to go, this lover of powerful song,
bowing my head, companionless.

23. Y Rhugl Groen

Fal yr oeddwn, fawl rwyddaf,
y rhyw ddiwrnod o'r haf
dan wŷdd rhwng mynydd a maes
yn gorllwyn fy nyn geirllaes,
dyfod a wnaeth, nid gwaeth gwad,
lle'r eddewis, lloer ddiwad.
Cydeistedd, cywiw destun,
amau o beth, mi a bun;
cyd-draethu, cyn henu hawl,
geiriau â bun ragorawl.
A ni felly, anhy oedd,
yn deall serch ein deuoedd,
yn celu murn, yn cael medd,
encyd awr yn cydorwedd,
dyfod a wnaeth, noethfaeth nych,
dan gri, rhyw feistri fystrych,
salw ferw fach sain gwtsach sail
o begor yn rhith bugail;
a chanto'r oedd, cyhoedd cas,
rugl groen flin gerngrin gorngras.
Canodd, felengest westfach,
y rhugl groen; och i'r hegl grach!
Ac yno cyn digoni
gwiw fun a wylltiodd; gwae fi!
Pan glybu hon, fron fraenglwy,
nithio'r main, ni thariai mwy.
Dan Grist ni bu dôn o Gred
can oer enw, cyn erwined.
Cod ar ben ffon yn sonio,
cloch sain o grynfain a gro.
Crwth cerrig Seisnig yn sôn
crynedig mewn croen eidion.
Cawell teirmil o chwilod,
callor dygyfor, du god.

23. The Rattle Bag

Upon a day (o easiest praise!)
in summer, when I found myself
under green trees between mountain and meadow
in ambush for my soft-worded girl,
she came, I'll not deny it,
the undoubted moon, to the promised place.
We sat together (splendid theme!)
not yet agreed, the girl and I,
and whilst this freedom was still mine
I conferred with the excellent girl.
Whilst we were thus, and she still shy,
realizing each other's love,
hiding the wrong and finding mead,
lying together the space of an hour,
there came, cold food for pining,
with a foul competitor of a cry,
a sorry little boiling sound from a bag's bottom,
from some beast in the form of a shepherd.
He had with him, notorious evil,
a nasty, shrivel-cheeked, dry-horned rattle bag.
He played this yellow-paunched prowler,
this rattle bag with its scabbed shank.
And so, o before satiety,
the worthy girl took fright,
for when she of the frail-wounded breast
heard the winnowed stones, she stayed no longer.
Under Christ, no Christian accent
with a cold name was ever so harsh;
a sounding bag at a stick's end,
a ringing bell of pebbles and grit,
a stony English instrument singing
quaveringly in a bullock's hide,
a cradle of three thousand chafers,
a hissing cauldron, a black bag,

Ceidwades gwaun, cydoes gwellt,
groenddu, feichiog o grynddellt.
Cas ei hacen gan heniwrch,
cloch ddiawl, a phawl yn ei ffwrch;
greithgrest garegddwyn grothgro,
yn gareiau byclau y bo.
Oerfel i'r carl gwasgarlun,
Amen, a wylltiodd fy mun.

a meadow guard, a companion of straw,
black-skinned, pregnant with splinters,
whose accent an old roebuck hates,
the devil's bell with a pole in her fork,
scar-crested, stone-bearing pebble-womb,
may it make thongs for buckles!
And a coldness on the scattering churl
(Amen!) who frightened away my girl!

24. Marwnad Lleucu Llwyd

Llyma haf llwm i hoywfardd,
a llyma fyd llwm i fardd.
Nid oes yng Ngwynedd heddiw
na lloer, na llewych, na lliw,
er pan rodded, trwydded trwch,
dan lawr dygn dyn loer degwch.
Y ferch wen o'r dderw brennol,
arfaeth ddig yw'r fau i'th ôl.
Cain ei llun, cannwyll Wynedd,
cyd bych o fewn caead bedd,
f'enaid, cyfod i fyny,
egor y ddaearddor ddu,
gwrthod wely tywod hir
a gwrtheb f'wyneb, feinir.
Mae yma hoywdra hydraul
uwch dy fedd, huanwedd haul,
ŵr prudd ei wyned hebod,
Llywelyn Goch, gloch dy glod;
udfardd yn rhodio adfyd
ydwyf, gweinidog nwyf gwyd;
myfi fun, mwyfwy fonedd,
echdoe a fûm uwch dy fedd
yn gollwng deigr llideigrbraff
ar hyd yr wyneb yn rhaff;
tithau, harddlun y fun fud,
o'r tewbwll ni'm atebud;
tawedog ddwysog ddiserch,
ti addawsud, y fud ferch,
fwyn dy sud, fando sidan,
f'aros, y ddyn loywdlos lân,
oni ddelwn, gwn y gwir,
ardwy hyder, o'r deheudir.

24. The Death of Lleucu Llwyd

It's a sad summer for a lively poet
and a sad world for him.
There is in Gwynedd to-day
nor moon, nor light, nor colour,
since was put (unlucky journey!)
the moon's beauty under hard earth.
O girl in your oak chest,
my fate is bitter without you.
Fine of form, candle of Gwynedd,
though you be in the grave's keeping,
my soul, bestir yourself,
open the black earth-door,
reject the long bed of gravel
and come to meet me, maiden.
There is here above your grave
(o brief beauty of sunny face!)
a sad-faced man who lacks you,
Llywelyn Goch, bell of your praise,
a wailing poet walking in affliction,
servant to passion's vigour.
O girl of growing excellence,
I was yesterday[1] above your grave
letting fall great streams of tears
in a rope along my face;
but you, fair image of a dumb girl,
gave me no answer from the dark pit,
loveless, profoundly speechless.
O silent girl, sweet-mannered,
bright, pretty one in a silk shroud,
you promised to wait for me
until I came from the south,
and that's the truth, the guard of trust.

---

[1] Literally, 'The day before yesterday', but this is not so easy to put into a line as
the Welsh word *echdoe*.

Ni chiglef, sythlef seithlud,
air ond y gwir, feinir fud,
iawndwf rhianedd Indeg,
onid hyn o'th enau teg.
Trais mawr, ac ni'm dawr am dŷ,
torraist amod trist ymy.
Tydi sydd, mau gywydd gau,
ar y gwir, rywiog eiriau;
celwyddog wyf, cul weddi,
celwyddlais a soniais i.
Mi af o Wynedd heddiw,
ni'm dawr pa fan, loywgan liw,
fy mun wyrennig ddigawn,
pe bait fyw, myn Duw, nid awn.
Pa le y caf, ni'm doraf, dioer,
dy weled, wendw wiwloer,
ar fynydd, sathr Ofydd serch,
Olifer, yr oleuferch?
Llwyr y diheuraist fy lle,
Lleucu, deg waneg wiwne,
rhiain loywgain oleugain,
rhy gysgadur mewn mur main.
Cyfod i orffen cyfedd,
i edrych a fynnych fedd,
at dy fardd, ni chwardd ychwaith
erot dalm, euraid dalaith;
dyred ffion ei deurudd
i fyny o'r pridd-dy prudd.
Anial yw ôl camoleg,
nid rhaid twyll, fy neudroed teg
yn bwhwman rhag annwyd
ynghylch dy dŷ, Lleucu Llwyd.
A genais, lugorn Gwynedd,
o eiriau gwawd, eiry ei gwedd,
llef drioch, llaw fodrwyaur,
Lleucu, moliant fu it, f'aur;
â'r genau hwn gwn ganmawl,
a ganwy, tra fwy, o fawl,
f'enaid, hoen geirw afonydd,

O straight, unhindered cry, I never heard
a lying word, my silent maiden,
true formed Indeg of girls,
from your sweet lips before.
A great blow to me, and I don't care where
I go, the sadness of your breach of faith.
No, you are true, it is my poem,
with its facile words, that's false.
I'm a liar, prayers are narrow,
I used a lying voice.
I'll go from Gwynedd to-day
no matter where, bright-coloured one,
my very lively one, and yet
if you still lived, by God, I would not go!
Where shall I, I don't care where,
see you again, my moon-fair girl?
Will it be on Mount Olivet,
where Ovid's love is trampled on?
You have made sure my place,
Lleucu, lovely, heavenly-fair wave,
dear-bright, fair-shining girl
oversleeping within your stone walls.
Get up to end the banquet,
to see whether you want the grave,
to your poet who no longer laughs
any more because of you, my gold chaplet.
Come, you of the cheeks of rose,
up from the gloomy earth-house!
A wilderness is the track,
this is the truth, of my true feet
walking to and fro in the cold
about your house, Lleucu Llwyd.
All the poetry I have sung,
lantern of Gwynedd, snow-featured,
gold-ringed hand, each triple-sighed cry
was praise of you, Lleucu my gold.
These lips know how to praise;
the praise I'll sing whilst I'm alive,
my soul, my love, my river-ripple colour,

fy nghariad, dy farwnad fydd.
Cymhennaidd groyw loyw Leucu,
cymyn f'anwylddyn fun fu:
ei henaid, grair gwlad Feiriawn,
i Dduw Dad, addewid iawn;
a'i mwyngorff, eiliw mangant,
meinir i gysegrdir sant;
dyn pellgŵyn, doniau peillgalch
a da byd i'r gŵr du balch;
a'i hiraeth, cywyddiaeth cawdd,
i minnau a gymynnawdd.
Lleddf ddeddf ddeuddawn ogyfuwch,
Lleucu dlos, lliw cawod luwch,
pridd a main, glain galarchwerw,
a gudd ei deurudd, a derw.
Gwae fi drymed y gweryd
a'r pridd ar feistres y pryd;
gwae fi fod arch i'th warchae
a thŷ main rhof a thi mae;
Gwae fi'r ferch wen o Bennal,
breuddwyd dig, briddo dy dâl!
Clo dur derw, galarchwerw gael,
a daear, deg ei dwyael,
a thromgad ddôr, a thrymgae,
a llawr maes rhof a'r lliw mae,
a chlyd fur a chlo dur du
a chlicied—yn iach, Leucu.

shall be your funeral song.
My dainty, clear, bright Lleucu,
my loved one's legacy was this:
her soul, Meirionnydd's jewel,
to God the Father, a true promise;
and her sweet body of fine flour hue
virgin to the saint's holy ground;
a faultless person, flour-white gifts
and the world's wealth to the black, proud one;
and, longing for her, she left to me
my song of resentful sorrow.
O mournful custom, two equal gifts
of earth and stone and oak now hide
her cheeks, the jewel of my bitter woe,
sweet Lleucu, of driven-snow colour.
Woe's me, the weight of gravel
and earth on beauty's mistress!
Woe's me, a coffin guards you
and a stone house between us two!
Woe is me, fair girl of Pennal,
and hateful dream that your brow should be earthed!
A hard oak case, o bitter sad lot,
and earth, o fair of feature,
and a heavy door, a heavy barrier,
a floor of field between her form and me,
a sheltering wall, a black steel lock
and a latch; goodbye, my Lleucu!

25. Y Llafurwr

Pan ddangoso, rhyw dro rhydd,
pobl y byd, peibl lu bedydd,
garbron Duw, cun eiddun oedd,
gwiw iaith ddrud, eu gweithredoedd
ar ben Mynydd, lle'i bydd barn
i gyd, Olifer gadarn,
llawen fydd chwedl diledlaes
llafurwr, tramwywr maes.
O rhoddes, hael yw'r hoywdduw,
offrwm a'i ddegwm i Dduw,
enaid da yna uniawn
a dâl i Dduw, dyly ddawn.
Hawdd i lafurwr hoywddol
hyder ar Dduw Nêr yn ol.
O gardod, drwy gywirdeb,
o lety, ni necy neb.
Ni rydd farn eithr ar arnawdd,
ni châr yn ei gyfar gawdd.
Ni ddeily rhyfel, ni ddilyn,
ni threisia am ei dda ddyn.
Ni bydd ry gadarn arnam,
ni yrr hawl gymedrawl gam,
nid addas ond ei oddef;
nid bywyd, nid byd heb ef.
Gwn mai digrifach ganwaith
gantho, modd digyffro maith,
gaffel, ni'm dawr heb fawr fai,
yr aradr crwm a'r irai,
no phed fai, pan dorrai dŵr,
yn rhith Arthur anrheithiwr.
Ni cheffir eithr o'i weithred
aberth Crist i borthi cred.
Bywyd ni chaiff, ni beiwn,
pab nac ymherawdr heb hwn,

25. *The Ploughman*

When the world's folk, one day of freedom,
the lively host of Christendom,
show their works before God
the beloved Lord (fine true words)
on the great mountain of Olivet,
where they will all be judged,
the labourer, the meadow traveller,
will tell a simple, cheerful tale.
The lively God is generous;
if a man has given God offering and tithe,
then a good soul directly
he'll pay to God and merit bliss.
The worker in the bright meadow
easily trusts to the Lord God.
Most properly his almsgiving
and hospitality are for all.
He'll speak his mind only on ploughs;
he hates dissension where he works.
He'll make and follow no war,
he'll oppress no one for his goods,
he's never brutal with us
nor will he pursue false claims.
Suffering is his seemly way,
yet there's no life without him.
He finds it many times pleasanter,
and I think no worse of him,
to grip in his placid way
the crooked plough and the goad
than if he were wrecking a tower
in the guise of a ravaging Arthur.
Without his work there's no
Christ's sacrifice to feed our faith,
and without him no pope
or emperor can keep alive,

na brenin haelwin hoywlyw,
dien ei bwyll, na dyn byw.
Lusudarus hwylus hen
a ddywod fal yn ddien,
'Gwyn ei fyd, trwy febyd draw,
a ddeily aradr â'i ddwylaw.'
Crud rhwyg fanadl gwastadlaes,
cryw mwyn a ŵyr creiaw maes.
Cerir ei glod, y crair glwys,
crehyr a'i hegyr hoywgwys;
cawell tir gŵydd rhwydd yrhawg,
calltrefn urddedig cylltrawg;
ceiliagwydd erwi gwyddiawn,
cywir o'i grefft y ceir grawn.
Cnwd a gyrch mewn cnodig âr,
cnyw diwael yn cnoi daear.
E fynn ei gyllell a'i fwyd
a'i fwrdd dan fôn ei forddwyd.
Gŵr â'i anfodd ar grynfaen,
gwas a fling a'i goes o'i flaen.
Ystig fydd beunydd ei ben,
ystryd iach is traed ychen.
Aml y canai ei emyn,
ymlid y fondid a fyn.
Un dryllwraidd dyffrynnaidd ffrwyth,
yn estyn gwddw anesmwyth;
gwas pwrffil aneiddil nen,
gwasgarbridd gwiw esgeirbren.
Hu Gadarn, feistr hoyw giwdawd,
brenin a roes gwin er gwawd,
amherawdr tir a moroedd,
cwnstabl aur Constinobl oedd;
daliodd ef wedi diliw
aradr gwaisg arnoddgadr gwiw;
ni cheisiodd, naf iachusoed,
fwriwr aer, fara erioed
eithr, da oedd ei athro,
o'i lafur braisg, awdur bro,
er dangos, eryr dawngoeth,

no wine-giving, sprightly king
of notable prudence, no living man.
The useful old Elucidarium
put it thus happily,
'Blessed is he who through his youth
holds in his hands the plough.'
It's a cradle tearing the smooth long broom,
a fishing basket lacing the field,
a holy image of dear praise,
a heron opening a quick furrow,
a basket for the wild earth, now to be tamed
in honoured, coultered order;
a gander of the wild acres,
grain will come of its true skill.
It fetches crops from the rich earth,
it's a good beast biting the ground.
It must have its knife and its board
and its food right under its thigh.
It goes unwillingly through stones,
it skins the field with leg outstretched.
It's head is ever employed
on a fair way beneath oxen's feet.
It has often sung its hymn,
it loves to follow the plough chain.
A root-breaker of valley growth,
it stretches a stiff neck out;
tough-headed train-bearer,
its wooden shank scatters the earth.
Hu Gadarn, lord of a lively people,
a king who gave wine for verse,
emperor of land and seas,
Constantinople's golden constable,
after defeat took up
the nimble, fine-beamed plough,
for this hale, host-scattering lord,
this great leader never sought bread
but, so well instructed was he,
by his own labour. This gifted eagle
wished to show to the proud

i ddyn balch a difalch doeth,
bod yn orau, nid gau gair,
ungrefft gan y Tad iawngrair,
arwydd mai hyn a oryw,
aredig, dysgedig yw.
Ffordd y mae cred a bedydd
a phawb yn cynnal y ffydd,
llaw Dduw cun, gorau un gŵr,
llaw Fair dros bob llafurwr.

and to the wisely humble that
in the true-jewelled Father's sight
one craft was best, a sign of triumph,
that ploughing is a scholarship.
Where there's belief and baptism
and everyone upholding the faith,
the Lord God's hand on this best of men
and Mary's hand on every ploughman.

26. Syr Hywel y Fwyall

A welai neb a welaf
yn y nos, a iawn a wnaf,
pan fwyf, mwyaf poen a fu,
yn hunaw anian henu?
Cyntaf y gwelaf mewn gwir
caer fawrdeg acw ar fordir
a chastell gwych gorchestawl
a gwŷr ar fyrddau a gwawl
a glasfor wrth fur glwysfaen
a geirw am groth tŵr gwrm graen;
a cherdd chwibenygl a chod,
gwawr hoenus, a gŵr hynod;
rhianedd, nid rhai anoyw,
yn gwau y sidan glân gloyw;
gwŷr beilch yn chwarae, gaer barth,
tawlbwrdd a secr uwch talbarth;
a gŵr gwynllwyd, Twrch Trwyd trin,
nawswyllt yn rhoi'i farneiswin
mewn gorflwch aur goreuryn
o'i law yn fy llaw fellŷn;
ac ystondardd hardd hirddu
yn nhâl tŵr, da filwr fu,
a thri blodeuyn gwyn gwiw
o'r unllun, dail arianlliw.
Eres nad oes henuriad
ar lawr Gwynedd wleddfawr wlad
o gwbl a allo gwybod
petwn lle mynnwn 'y mod.
'Oes,' heb yr un, 'syberw wyd,
breuddwydiaw obry'dd ydwyd.
Y wal deg a weli di,
da dyddyn y doud iddi,
a'r gaer eglur ar greiglofft
a'r garreg rudd ar gwr grofft,

26. Sir Hywel of the Axe

Would anyone see what I see
in the night (I'll make amends)
when, in the greatest pain that is,
I sleep as an old man sleeps?
For first I truly see
a fine great sea-fronting fort,
with a splendidly built keep,
men on the platforms, a rampart,
and the blue sea at its fair stone base,
with foam to the swelling of the blue-grained tower,
the song of fifes and bagpipes,
a joyful dawn and a notable man;
then girls, far from unlively,
weaving the shining, lovely silk;
proud men at the fort's high table
playing backgammon and chequers;
a pale, grey man, the boar of battle,
wild-natured, gives me his sweet wine
in finest golden goblet
thus from his hand into mine;
and a fine long black standard
above the tower (a good soldier was he),
with three white worthy flowers
of the same form, with silver leaves.
Strange that there is no elder
in Gwynedd's great feasting land
who is now able to tell me
whether I am where I wish to be.
One answers, 'Yes, proud fellow,
you're dreaming over there.
The fair wall that you see,
the good homestead you'd come to,
the bright fort on its height of rock
and the red rock at the croft corner,

hon yw Cruciath a'i gwaith gwiw—
hen adail honno ydiw.
A'r gŵr llwyd cadr paladrddellt
yw Syr Hywel, mangddel mellt,
a'i wraig, Syr, wregys euraid,
Hywel, iôn rhyfel yn rhaid;
a'i llawforynion ton teg—
ydd oeddynt hwy bob ddeuddeg
yn gwau sidan glân gloywliw
wrth haul belydr drwy'r gwydr gwiw.
Tau olwg, ti a welud
ystondardd, ys hardd o sud;
pensel Syr Hywel yw hwn;
myn Beuno, mae'n ei bennwn
tri fflŵr-de-lis, orris erw,
yn y sabl, nid ansyberw.'
Anian mab Gruffudd, rudd rôn,
ymlaen at ei elynion,
yn minio gwayw mewn eu gwaed,
anniweirdrefn, iôn eurdraed;
Ysgythrwr cad, aets goethrudd,
esgud i'r aer, ysgwyd rudd;
Ysgithredd baedd ysgethrin
asgwrn hen yn angen in.
Pan rodded, trawsged rhwysgainc,
y ffrwyn ym mhen brenin Ffrainc,
barbwr fu fal mab Erbin
â gwayw a chledd, trymwedd trin;
eilliaw â'i law a'i allu
bennau a barfau y bu;
a gollwng gynta gallai
y gwaed tros draed—trist i rai.
Annwyl fydd gan ŵyl Einiort,
aml ei feirdd, a mawl i'w fort.
Gwarden yw, garw deunawosgl,
a maer ar y drawsgaer drosgl;
cadr gwrser yn cadw garsiwn,
cadw'r tir yn hir a wna hwn.

this is Cricieth of fine structure,
it's that old citadel.
The grey man, the great spear-shatterer,
is Sir Hywel, lightning's gun,
with his wife of golden girdle,
Sir Hywel, lord of needful war,
and her fair-skinned handmaidens,
ranged there twelve by twelve,
weaving the bright-hued fair silk
in the shafts of the sun through worthy glass.
And in your vision you saw
a standard of splendid sort:
this is Sir Hywel's streamer
and, by Beuno, in this pennon
are three fleur-de-lys embroidered
proudly in their sable ground.'
The nature of bloody-speared Gruffudd's son
led him to his enemies
to sharpen his lance in their blood
savagely, this golden-footed lord,
carver of battle, fine red H,
speedy to war, the bloody shield,
tusks of a fearful boar,
an old backbone to us in our need.
When he put (what a check for pomp!)
a bridle on the French King's head,
he was a barber like Erbin's son,
with lance and sword, both heavy in battle;
he shaved, with his hand and strength,
the heads and beards he met,
letting flow, as fast as he could,
blood over feet, a grief for some.
He will be loved by the gentle romancer,[1]
his poets are many, his table's praised.
He's warden, an eighteen-pointed stag,
and keeper of the huddled town;
a brave warhorse keeping the garrison,
long will he keep the land.

[1] Who may Einiort be unless Eilhart? Iolo's knowledge and interests are wide and unpredictable.

Cadw'r bobl mewn cadair bybyr,
cadw'r castell, gwell yw na gwŷr,
cadw dwy lins, ceidwad Loensiamp;
cadw'r ddwywlad, cadw'r gad, cadw'r gamp;
cadw'r mordarw cyda'r mordir,
cadw'r mordrai, cadw'r tai, cadw'r tir;
cadw'r gwledydd oll, cadw'r gloywdwr,
a chadw'r gaer: iechyd i'r gŵr!

He'll protect the people in his strong seat,
he'll hold the castle, he's better than an army,
he'll hold two frontiers, this keeper of Longchamps;
he'll hold the two lands and war and its reward;
he'll keep the walrus at the shore,
he'll keep the tides, the halls, the land;
he'll hold all lands and the bright tower,
he'll hold the fort: health to the man!

27. Hud a Lliw y Byd

Un fodd yw'r byd, cyngyd cêl,
â phaentiwr delw â phwyntel,
yn paentiaw delwau lawer,
a llu o saint â lliw sêr.
Fal hudol â'i fol hoywdew
yn bwrw hud, i angwr glud glew
dangos a wna, da diddim
dwys ei dâl, lle nid oes dim.
Felly'r byd hwn, gwn ganwaith,
hud a lliw, nid gwiw ein gwaith.

Mae'r byd oll? Mawr bu dwyllwr.
Mae Addaf fu gyntaf gŵr?
Mae Rwling frenin Corstinobl?
Mae'r ddau mawr Babau? Mae'r bobl?
Mae Sulus frenin Susil?
Mae feirdd Ewropa? Mae fil?
Alexander a dderyw,
Ector, Arthur, eglur yw.
Mae Gwenhwyfar, gwawn hoywwedd,
merch Gogfran gawr, fawr a fedd,
a'r sidan, eres ydiw,
a'r gwallt llawn perles aur gwiw?
Mae Tegfedd ryfedd yrhawg,
coelferch Owain Cyfeiliawg?
Mae Firain, eurfain wryd
o Ffrainc, oedd decaf ei phryd?
Mae Herod greulon honnaid?
Mae Siarlymaen o'r blaen blaid?
Mae Fasil fab? Mae Foesen?
Mae Brutus fab Sulus hen?
Mae Owain, iôr archfain oedd?
Mae Risiard frenin? Mae'r oesoedd?

27. *The Illusion of this World*

Its purpose hidden, the world is like
an image painter with his brush
painting many images
and a host of saints in star colour.
Like a fat-bellied magician
casting a spell, to a fervent, brave warrior
it shows something where nothing is,
worthless stuff which is bought dear.
That's this world, I know it well,
magic and colour; our work's of no avail.

Where's all the world? It's been a deceiver.
Where's Adam, the first man?
Where's Rulling,[1] Constantinople's king?
Where are the two great popes and their retinues?
Where's Julius, King of Sicily;
the poets of Europe and a thousand more?
Alexander has perished,
and Hector and Arthur, that's clear.
Where's Guinevere, gossamer-featured,
daughter of giant Gogfran of great dominion,
and the silk that was so wonderful
and the hair full of beads of fitting gold?
Where now will marvellous Tegwedd be,
the love of Owain Cyfeiliog?
Where's Vivien, the slim golden armful
from France, whose face was fairest?
Where's Herod, of famous cruelty?
Where's Charlemagne of the vanguard party?
Where's young Basil? Where is Moses?
Where's Brutus, son of old Julius?
Where's Owain, the slim-waisted lord?
Where is King Richard? Where are the ages?

[1] I have failed to trace Rulling and simply anglicise the name.

Mae'r haelion bobl? Mae'r helynt?
Mae'r gwyrda fu Gymry gynt,
mae'r perchen tai? Mae'r parchau
yn fab a welais yn fau?
Ni ŵyr cennad goeladwy
na herod gwynt eu hynt hwy.
A'r undawns, gwn ei wrandaw,
i ninnau diau y daw.
Heliwn olud ehudwaith;
hud a lliw, nid gwiw ein gwaith.

Anniweiriaf fu Ddafydd;
Selyf ddoeth, salw fu ei ddydd.
Dyryseinia dros annerch,
Duc Iorc a rôi forc i ferch.
Maent hwy a'u gwragedd heddiw,
a'u mawredd gwych a'u medd gwiw?
Mae'r hud iaith? Mae'r rhai doethion?
Mae'r saith gelfyddyd? Mae'r sôn?
Mae Catw ddoeth? Mae Cytal?
Mae'r saith ddysg Fferyll, mawr sâl?
Er ei gallter, medd gwerin,
a'i fawr gelfyddyd o'i fin,
a'i hoced mawr a'i hwcian,
aeth i'r ddaear fal gwâr gwan.
Er eu dewred, wŷr diriaid,
a'u balchedd rhyfedd a'u rhaid,
yn ddiddim, awgrim ograff,
i'r pridd ydd aethant, wŷr praff.
O'r pridd y doetham er praw,
i'r pridd ydd awn, er pruddaw.
Afraid i ddyn fryd ar dda
a'i ryfig a'i wareufa
a'i dolciog gorff a'i dalcen
a'i bwys o bridd a'i bais bren;
ac wythgant, meddant i mi,
o bryfed yn ei brofi.
Had daear ar hyd dwywaith;
hud a lliw, nid gwiw ein gwaith.

Where are the generous ones and their concerns?
Where are the worthies of old Wales,
the house-holders? Where's the reverence
which as a youth belonged to me?
No credible messenger,
no herald of the wind knows where they are.
The same dance, I hear it come,
will without doubt be ours.
We gather a fortune, a fool's task;
magic and colour, our work's of no avail.

David was most unchaste;
wise Solomon's day was vile.
It echoes over salutation,
York's Duke would give a girl a mark.
Where are they and their women to-day,
their great splendour, their fine mead?
Where are the spells, where the wise ones,
where the seven arts and their fame?
Where's the wise Cato, and Catiline,
and the helpful, seven-wisdomed Virgil?[1]
In spite of his wisdom, people say,
and the great science of his speech
and his tricks and huckstering,
to earth, a tame weakling, he went.
Though those bad men were brave,
strangely proud and demanding,
quite clearly, though strong, they went
as nothing into earth.
From earth we came to our testing;
to earth, though we mourn it, we must go.
Useless to man is love of goods,
his daring and playfulness,
with a battered body and forehead,
with a weight of earth, a tunic of wood,
and, if they tell me truly,
eight hundred worms tasting him.
Earth's seed is now in two lengths;
magic and colour, our work's of no avail.

[1] Virgil was more famous as a wizard than as a poet in the Middle Ages.

Pan ddêl Crist, poen ddial cred,
parth y gaer porth agored
Dduw Sul i farn yn ddisom
ar dda a drwg, a'r ddôr drom,
rhai'n crynu fal maeddu mab,
eraill yn llawen arab;
rhai a gaiff nefoedd i gyd,
rhai boenau, rhyfawr benyd.
Yno y gwelwn, iôn gwiwlaith,
hud a lliw, nid gwiw ein gwaith.

O avenging pain of faith! When Christ
comes to the open castle gate
one Sunday as infallible judge
of good and bad, at that sad door
some will cringe like a beaten boy,
some will be gay and merry;
some will receive all heaven,
some pain, excess of punishment.
Then, Lord of worthy Death, shall we see
magic and colour, that our work's of no avail.

28. Cywydd Merch

Dyn wyf yn cerdedd y nos,
(dedwyddach oedd dŷ diddos)
dyn hurt am gerdded yn hwyr,
dros hyn Duw a ro synnwyr.
Du arnaf ydyw oernos,
Duw, dy nawdd, dued y nos!
Dyn ni bu, a'r dyno bach
dan bared, wyneb oerach.
Deffro fun, differ f'enaid,
dyn Duw blin sy dan dy blaid.
Dyro, ti a gai deirhan,
dy wisg, dy gardod i wan,
dy lety, dy law ataf,
dy deg gorff, dywed a'i caf.
Dy fwyn air er dy fonedd,
dy fin fal diod o fedd.
Dy faeth, dy gellwair, dy fodd,
dy feinael a'm difwynodd.
Dy laeswallt fal dy lusael,
dy drem fal dued yr ael;
dy bryd fal dillad broidyr,
du a gwyn i hudo gwŷr;
dy wyneb fal od unnos,
dy wrid fal bagad o ros.
Dy garu di a gerais,
dy gas im nis dygai Sais.
Dig wyf yn arwain dy gerdd
dan fargod yn ofergerdd;
drwy ffenestr dyro ffunen
dy fam hael i doi fy mhen.
Dy gerdd ymhob gwlad a gaf,
dy bwyth nis diobeithiaf.
Dy garu i'm digio 'rwy;
diseml wyd, disyml ydwy.

28. *To a Girl*

I'm a man walking the night,
a snug house would be happier;
a stupid man late walking;
for this may God give him sense!
Cold night is black upon me:
God, your help, how black the night!
Sorry little wretch under a wall,
there was never a colder face.
Wake up, girl, protect my soul,
a weary, godly man's under your wall.
Give, you'll get threefold payment,
your garment as alms to the weak,
your lodging, your hand towards me,
your lovely body, say, shall I have it?
Your sweet word from your nobleness,
your lip, like a drink of mead?
Your nurture, gaiety and pleasure,
your slim brow have ruined me.
Your soft hair, your bilberry brow,
your glance, how dark your eyebrow!
Your colouring like monks' vestments,
black and white, bewitches men;
your face like last night's snow,
your blush a bunch of roses.
I have loved loving you:
no Englishman would be so cruel to me.
Indignantly I bear your song,
under eaves vainly singing.
Pass your kind mother's kerchief
through the window to roof my head!
Your song will I sing everywhere
and not despair of your requiting.
I love you to spite myself;
you courtly and I artless.

Digon caead yw d'ogylch,
dyn deg wyt, nawdd Duw'n dy gylch!
Dig wy yn arwain dy gân;
dygum gas, dwg im gusan.
Dy gyngor rhag dig angen
da fydd ei gael, dy fodd, Gwen.

Your precincts are well locked,
you're lovely; may God be about you!
Indignantly I bear your poem,
I've been ill-treated, give me a kiss!
Your counsel against urgent wrath
will be good, and your consent, my Gwen.

29. I Wallt Merch

A ga'i'r ferch a garaf i?
A ga'i lwyn y goleuni,
a'i brig sirig fal seren
awyr, a physt aur o'i phen?
Tân draig yn tywynnu drws,
tair tid fal y Tŵr Tewdws
Enynnu bydd yn un berth
o nen gwalc yn un goelcerth.
Banhadlen neu fedwen fawr,
benfelen bun o Faelawr.
Lleng eiliw llu angylion,
llawer cainc yw llurig hon;
penwn o blu paun un blaid,
perth hir fal y porth euraid;
hyn o wallt hoyw iawn ei wedd,
haul rhin, hual rhianedd.
Pawb a ŵyr, pe bai eurych,
pwy biau'r gwallt pybyr gwych.
Y mae a pheth am ei phen
yr haf fal y Rhiw Felen.
Teg o dwf yw twyg y dyn,
tent haul fal tannau telyn;
brig ŷd wedi'i beri i gau,
brwyn bilion fal bron belau;
peunes yn dwyn pob unawr
banadl wallt o ben hyd lawr;
gwydn gwefr i gyd yn gwau,
gold ŷd fal gwiail didau;
coed yw ei gwallt cyd a gwŷdd,
coron wiail cŵyr newydd.
Eginodd gwaith y gwenyn
egin tes o gnawd dyn,
saffrwm ar lysiau effros,

29. *A Girl's Hair*

Shall I have the girl I love?
Shall I have the grove of light,
with her silken, starry hair
in golden columns from her head,
dragon fire lighting up a door,
three chains like the Milky Way?
She sets alight in one bush
a roof of hair like a bonfire.
Yellow broom or a great birch tree
is this gold-topped girl of Maelor.
A host coloured like angels,
her armour's many-branched,
a peacock-feather pennon,
a tall bush like the golden door,
all this lively looking hair
virtued like the sun, fetter of girls.
Anyone would know, were he a goldsmith,
who owns this fine strong hair.
In summer she has on her head
something like the Golden Hillside.
This fair growth is the girl's garment,
a tent for the sun, or harp strings,
ears of corn closed in above,
reed peelings like a marten's breast;
a peahen constantly carrying
hair of broom from head to ground,
a noose of woven amber,
the gold of corn like twig-chains;
her hair's a tree-high woodland,
a twig-crown of new wax.
Labour of bees has ripened
the seeds of warmth from a girl's flesh,
saffron on the herb eyebright,

sirian aur fal sêr y nos.[1]
Da fu'r rhimp ar dwf yrhawg,
dyfrwelltir, deifrwallt eurawg;
lleisw a'i gwlych fal llysiau glân,
llinos iad, llwyn o sidan.
Ysgub fanadl Fair Fadlen
yw'r rhimp aur yn rhwymo pen;
ac yn rhudd o gawn rhyddwallt,
yn aur y gwisg own o'r gwallt.
Ei dwy gofl ydyw i gyd
o do aur a dau wryd;
llywethau teg llwyth iad dyn,
llin ymlaen llwyn melynyn.
Aur yw'r llwyn o'i roi ar lled:
a fu lwyn cyn felyned?
Er mwyn bod o'r maen bedydd
ôl ar ei phen olew'r ffydd,
a rhoi i lwyn yr haul einioes,
rhyw lwyn dan yr haul nid oes.

[1] See footnote *YFN* p. 113.

cherries of gold, like the stars of night.
A good band round its coming growth,
fresh water-grass, golden water-hair,
lye water wets it like sweet herbs;
yellow-hammer head, bush of silk;
a sheaf of Mary Magdalen's broom
is the gold band that binds her hair.
If we let it down all glowing,
we'll forget hair in a golden garment.
It covers her two breasts
from its roof of gold in two fathoms,
fair ringlets, load of a girl's head,
flax before bush of yellow.
If spread out, the bush is gold:
was ever bush so yellow?
In order that from the christening font
the oil of faith should mark her head,
giving life to the sun's bush,
there's no such bush now under the sun.

30. Enwi'r Ferch

Gwrid mawr o gariad morwyn
y sydd nos a dydd i'm dwyn;
caru gwen fwnwgl hirwyn
heb wybod oll i bob dyn.
Y mae gwin im o'i genau,
y mae gwên hon i'm gwanhau.
Be rhôn bob awr i'w henwi,
nid oes dyn a'i hedwyn hi.
Annes unwaith a enwaf,
amod ag emod a gaf
ar ddyn dda ei llun a'i lliw;
ond odid emod ydyw.
Gwenhwyfar feddylgar fwyn,
Gwladus a'r gwefus ryfwyn,
Catrin, Gwenllian annerch,
Cari, Mallt, cywira merch,
Lleucu lliw briallu bron,
Lowri dan wiail irion;
mwyn yw cusan Myfanwy,
marfol iawn am Weirful wy;
mae cred Margared imi,
rhuddaur pell im ei rhodd hi.
Curo'r grudd, cywiro'r gred,
caru cusanu Sioned;
gwyllt isel yw fy ngolwg,
gorwedd â'm Tegwedd a'm dwg.
Gwan wyf, y mae gwayw yn fy iad,
mwy yw 'nghur am Angharad.
Mae saeth yn ei mynwes hir
yn oes tanw nis tynnir.
Seren dan y cyrs eurwallt,
selu rwy' Alswn i allt.
Mae meillion gwynion mewn gwydd,
mae ir fedw im a Morfudd.

30. Naming the Girl

The great warmth of a maiden's love
has me captive night and day;
loving a girl with a long bright mane
and keeping it a secret.
From her lips I get wine,
her smile enfeebles me.
If they took all time to name her,
yet no man would know her.
Annes first will I name;
I'll make a pact in gems
with a fine girl in colour and form;
yes, she is gems indeed.
Sweet pensive Guinevere,
Gwladus of the sugared lip,
Catherine, Gwenllian I'll greet,
Cari, Mallt, the properest girl,
Lleucu of hill primrose hue,
Lowri under green branches.
Soft is Myfanwy's kiss;
I'm at death's door for Gweirful;
Margaret's faith is mine,
she brings far-brought red gold.
I beat my cheek and keep my faith,
I love kissing my Janet;
wild and low is my look,
lying with Tegwedd has charmed me.
I'm weak, there's a spear in my skull,
my pain for Angharad grows greater.
There's an arrow in her deep bosom
which won't be drawn in a meteor's life.
A star under gold rushes of hair,
I spy out Alison for the wood.
In the woods there is white trefoil,
a green birch tree and Morfudd.

Alis, Isabel, Elen,
Efa, Nest fy nyn wen.
Y mae hyn wedi ei henwi,
ac un o hyn, gwen yw hi.

Alis, Isabel, Helen,
Eva or Nêst is my bright girl.
And now she has been named,
for one of these is the girl.

31. Marwnad Siôn Eos

Drwg i neb a drigo'n ôl
cost am un cas damweiniol;
y drwg lleia o'r drygwaith
yn orau oll yn yr iaith.
O wŷr, pam na bai orau,
o lleddid un na lladd dau?
Dwyn ein gelynwaed a wnaeth,
dial ein dwy elyniaeth.
Oedd oer ladd y ddeuwr lân
heb achos ond un bychan.
Er briwio'r gŵr, heb air gwad,
o'i farw ni bu fwriad.
Yr oedd y diffyg ar rai
am adladd mewn siawns medlai;
ymryson am yr oesau
a'r ing a ddaeth rhwng y ddau.
Oddi yna lladd y naill ŵr
a'i ddial, lladd y ddeuwr.
Y corff dros y corff os caid,
yr iawn oedd well i'r enaid.
Oedd, wedi, addewidion,
ei bwys o aur er byw Siôn.
Sorrais wrth gyfraith sarrug;
Swydd y Waun Eos a ddug.
Y swydd, pam na roit dan sêl
i'th Eos gyfraith Hywel?
Ar hwn wedi cael o rhain
ffrwythlonder cyfraith Lundain,
ni mynnen am ei einioes
noethu crair na thorri croes.
Y gŵr oedd dad y gerdd dant
yn oeswr nis barnasant;
deuddeg yn un od oeddyn,
Duw deg, ar fywyd y dyn.

31. The Death of Siôn Eos

It's hard for those left behind,
the trouble of a chance enmity;
the smallest of all crimes,
but the best man in all our tongue.
O men, why isn't it better,
if one is killed, not to kill two?
He took one enemy's blood,
avenged our dual enmity.
It was sad, the killing of two good men
for such a little cause!
He wounded, there's no denying,
but never meant to kill the man.
Somebody was at fault
for striking back in a chance mêlée.
Contention for generations
and the suffering that came between the two;
and so one man was killed
and vengeance takes the other.
Even if body paid for body
justice would be better for the soul.
Then came the promises—
his weight in gold to save Siôn's life.
I hate the churlish law;
the Chirk Lordship took a nightingale away.
O Lordship, why not under seal
apply Hywel's law to your Nightingale?
When they had put upon him
the fullness of London's law,
they would not, for his life's sake,
lay bare a relic or cut a cross.
And so they doomed to death
the man who was father of music;
the twelve were all agreed,
fair God, on the man's life.

Wedi Siôn nid oes synnwyr
da i gerdd na dyn a'i gŵyr;
torres braich tŵr eos brig,
torred mesur troed miwsig,
torred ysgol tŷ'r desgant,
torred dysg fal torri tant.
Oes mwy rhwng Euas a Môn
o'r dysg abl i'r disgyblion?
Rheinallt nis gŵyr ei hunan,
rhan gŵr er hynny a gân.
Fe aeth dy gymar yn fud,
yn dortwll[1] delyn Deirtud.
Ti y sy'n tewi â sôn,
telyn aur y telynorion.
Bu'n dwyn dan bob ewin dant,
bysedd llef gŵr neu basdant;[2]
myfyrdawd rhwng bawd a bys,
main a threbl mwyn â thribys.
Oes dyn wedï'r Eos deg
yn gystal a gân gosteg
a phrofiad neu ganiad gŵr,
a chwlwm ger bron uchelwr?
Pwy'r awron mewn puroriaeth,
pe na bai a wnâi, a wnaeth?
Ag atgas ni wn gytgerdd,
eisieu gwawd eos y gerdd.
Nid oes nac angel na dyn
nad ŵyl pan gano delyn.
Och heno rhag ei chanu,
wedï'r farn ar awdur fu.
Eu barn ym mhorth nef ni bydd,
Wŷr y Waun, ar awenydd.
Os iawn farn a fu arno,
yr un farn arnyn a fo.
Efô a gaiff ei fywyd,
nid o'u barn newidio byd.
Oes fy nyn y sy yn nos,
oes fy Nuw i Siôn Eos!

[1] Thus YFN, where W. J. Gruffydd directs our attention to a note on Teirtu's harp
in Lady Charlotte Guest's *Mabinogion* (*Kulhwch and Olwen*).
[2] GDE and YFN give *basant*.

Now Siôn's gone, there's no good sense
in music, nor master of it.
An arm felled the tree-top nightingale's tower;
the measure of music's foot was broken,
the school-house of descant was broken,
learning was broken like a string breaking.
Is there from Ewyas to Anglesey
learning left fit for learners?
Rheinallt himself doesn't know
and yet he sings a man's part;
his fellow has fallen silent
and Teirtu's harp is shattered.
You now are silent too,
golden harp of the harpists.
Each finger-nail held a string,
keys of the male voice or base note,
a meditation between thumb and finger,
mean and sweet treble from three fingers.
Is there, now Nightingale's gone,
his equal at playing a prelude,
an improvisation and manly song,
an air in a nobleman's presence?
What maker now in music
has anything but what he made?
Distastefully, I know no concord
without the song of music's Nightingale.
There is no angel or man
who'd not weep at his harp-playing.
O, let it not be played tonight,
now that its master is doomed!
O men of Chirk, your judgement won't avail
against the musician at Heaven's gate!
And if their judgement was just,
may the same doom fall upon them;
it's he who'll go to life,
not changing worlds at their verdict.
Life to my man who's in the night,
and God's life to John Nightingale!

32. Y Grawys

Y dydd o wynfyd Eiddig
er doe a ddaeth, yr ydwy'n ddig;
dydd a'i bwys fal diwedd byd
ar awenydd yw'r Ynyd;
dechreuad ffordd Paradwys,
Duw yn dwyn pawb dan eu pwys.
Deugain nieu maddeuaint
y sydd i weddiau saint;
f'Arglwydd, yn gyd â blwyddyn
y rhoed pob diwrnod o hyn.
Hir oedd ym', herwa ydd wyf,
dridiau'n y byd yr ydwyf.
Crefydd yr ancr o Rufain
ydyw'r mau fal awdur main;
cywir wyf yn eu crefydd,
cywir yw bun, caru bydd
gan roi fal Gwenerau yn'
grawysgwaith i'n goresgyn.
Yn iach fy rhiein feinwasg,
dillin pawb hyd Dduw Llun Pasg.
Nis gwelaf, nid af o dŷ
ati un nos hyd hynny.
Nid archaf gusan, f'annwyl,
mwy na dim[1] i'm enaid ŵyl.
Pan ddel y Pasg ar glasgoed,
bun a ddaw beunydd i oed;
nid amod wisgo damasg
dalu'r pwyth hyd wyliau'r Pasg.
Yno daw in' y dydd
a'i lonaid o lawenydd;
a Mai a haf lle mae hon
a chogau fel merch Wgon;
a phob bedwlwyn mewn manwallt

[1] Thus BDG. *MS Llanstephan* 133 gives *dyn.*

32. *From Lent to Summer*

The jealous husband's day of bliss
came yesterday to plague me;
Shrove-tide's a day that weighs
like the world's end on a poet.
The way to heaven opens,
God leads men under their loads;
forty days of forgiveness
there are for saintly prayers.
Lord, every single day
was doled out like a year.
Three days of this, an outlaw's fate,
are long for the world I live in.
The anchorite's faith from Rome
becomes mine, like an author of prayers;
in their faith I'm correct,
the girl's correct, she'll love,
giving us, like Fridays,
lenten tasks to subdue us.
Goodbye, my little slimwaist,
everyone's chaste till Easter Monday.
I'll not see her, nor for her leave
the house one night till then.
I'll not beg for a kiss, my dear,
nor anything for my bashful soul.
When Easter comes with its green trees,
the girl will meet me daily.
Is not the payment made through Easter
a covenant for damask wearing?
Then will come our day
with its plenitude of joy,
May and summer, where she is
and cuckoos like Gwgon's daughter;
each birchgrove in fine hair,

a phais wyrdd a phwys o wallt
ac ar ystryd a gyrs drain
siopeu lawnd fal Sieb Lundain;
llysiau mewn garddau a gwlith,
grawn gwin a grynau gwenith,
wybr eglur a môr briglas
a llen glud yn y llwyn glas
a lle ynial a llannerch
a changen feinwen o ferch
a gorffen cwbl o'n penyd
a threio'r bâr[1] a throi'r byd
a rhoi ein melltith yrhawg
ar y Gwanwyn oer gwynnawg.

[1] Thus BDG. *MS Llan.* 133 gives *badd*.

a green coat and a weight of hair,
and on the street of thorn stems
linen shops like London's Cheap;
herbs and dew in gardens,
berries for wine, ridges of wheat,
a clear sky, a blue-capped sea,
a snug screen in a green grove,
a lonely place in a glade
and a slim branch of a girl.
Then we'll end all our penance,
ebb out the pain and spin the world
and henceforth put our curses
on the chilly, windy Spring.

33. Marwnad Siôn y Glyn

Un mab oedd degan i mi,
Dwynwen, gwae'i dad o'i eni!
Gwae a edid o gudab
i boeni mwy heb un mab,
Fy nwy ais, farw fy nisyn,
y sy'n glaf am Siôn y Glyn.
Udo fyth yr ydwyf i
am benaig Mabinogi.
Afal pêr ac aderyn
a garai'r gwas, a gro gwyn;
bwa o flaen y ddraenen,
cleddau digon brau o bren;
ofni'r bib, ofni'r bwbach,
ymbil â'i fam am y bêl fach;
canu i bawb acen o'i ben,
canu io-o er cneuen;
gwneuthur moethau, gwenieitho,
sorri wrthyf i wnai fo
a chymod er ysglodyn
ac er dis a garai'r dyn.
Och, nad Siôn, fab gwirion gwâr,
sy'n ail oesi Sain Lasar!
Beuno a droes iddo saith
nefolion yn fyw eilwaith;
gwae eilwaith fy ngwir galon
nad oes wyth, rhwng enaid Siôn.
O Fair, gwae fi o'i orwedd,
a gwae fy ais gan ei fedd!
Yngo y saif angau Siôn
yn ddeufrath yn y ddwyfron.
Fy mab, fy muarth baban,
fy mron, fy nghalon, fy nghân,
fy mryd cyn fy marw ydoedd,
fy mardd doeth, fy moeth im oedd;

33. On the Death of his Son

One son was a jewel to me:
o Dwynwen, his father bewails his birth!
I have been left pain for love,
to ache for ever without a son.
My plaything is dead and my sides
are sick for Siôn y Glyn.
I moan continually
for a little story-book chieftain.
A sweet apple and a bird
the boy loved, and white pebbles,
a bow made of a thorn twig
and little brittle swords of wood.
He feared a pipe and a scarecrow
and begged his mother for a ball.
He'd sing for anyone,
singing io-o for a nut.
He'd make as though to flatter
and then fall out with me;
then make it up for a chip of wood
or a dice that he desired.
O, that Siôn, sweet innocent,
could live again like Lazarus.
Beuno brought seven heaven-dwellers
back again into this life.
Woe upon woe to my true heart
that Siôn's soul does not make eight.
O Mary, woe for his lying down
and woe to my side for his grave!
Siôn's death stands near me
like two barbs in my breast.
My son, child of my hearth,
my breast, my heart, my song,
my one delight before my death,
my knowing poet, my luxury.

fy nhegan oedd, fy nghannwyll,
fy enaid teg, fy un twyll;
fy nghyw yn dysgu fy nghân,
fy nghae Esyllt, fy nghusan;
fy nyth, gwae fi yn ei ôl,
fy ehedydd, fy hudol;
fy Siôn, fy mwa, fy saeth,
f'ymbiliwr, fy mabolaeth;
Siôn y sy'n danfon i'w dad
awch o hiraeth a chariad.
Yn iach wên ar fy ngenau,
yn iach chwerthin o'r min mau;
yn iach mwy ddiddanwch mwyn,
ac yn iach i gnau echwyn
ac yn iach bellach i'r bêl
ac yn iach ganu uchel;
ac yn iach fy nghâr arab
iso'n fy myw, Siôn fy mab.

my jewel, and my candle,
my sweet soul, my one betrayal,
my chick learning my song,
my chaplet of Iseult, my kiss,
my nest, (woe that he's gone!)
my lark, my little wizard.
My Siôn, my bow, my arrow,
my suppliant, my boyhood,
Siôn who sends to his father
a sharpness of longing and love.
No more smiles for my lips,
no more laughter from my mouth,
no more sweet entertainment,
no more begging for nuts,
no longer any playing ball
and no more singing aloud.
Farewell, whilst I live below,
my merry darling, my Siôn.

34. I Ofyn March

Gydag un a geidw Gwynedd
y cawn ar lan Conwy'r wledd,
abad tros wythwlad y sydd,
Aberconwy barc gwinwydd,
arglwydd yn rhoi gwledd yn rhad,
arfer ddwbl ar fwrdd abad;
powdrau yn nysglau y naill
a'r oraits i rai eraill.
Conwy, rhyd dyffryn cynnes,
cefn y ffrwd lle caf win ffres,
Glyn Grwst a glan Gaer Awstin,
glyn gwyrdd y galwynau gwin.
Tri phwys cegin y tywysog,
troi mae'r gwaith trwm ar ei gog;
tai aml am win, temlau medd,
trestl a bwtri osgedd;[1]
ar ei winoedd ar unwaith
yno bu ben am bob iaith.
Ple cyrchwn sesiwn y saint?
Gydag ef a'i gyd gwfaint,
gwŷr yn rhif gwerin Rhufain,
gwyn a rhudd yw gynau rhain.
Os gwyn ei fynwes a'i gob,
o'r un wisg yr â'n esgob.
Fe âi'r mab dan fur a main
be'i profid yn bab Rhufain.
Gwaith blin ac anoethineb
ymryson oll am ras neb;
hwynthwy mil o renti mân,
yntau fynnai rent Faenan.
Mae ar wyneb Meirionnydd
blaid i'r gŵr fel blodau'r gwŷdd.

[1] YFN conjectures *Trestl a bwtri i eistedd.* For variant readings in the MSS see YFN p. 146

34. To Ask for a Stallion

On Conwy bank have I been feasted
by one who is keeper of Gwynedd,
an abbot over eight regions,
Aberconwy's vine enclosure,
a lord who freely gives feasts,
doubly a habit at an abbot's table;
spices in one man's dish,
oranges in another's.
Conwy, ford of a temperate valley,
the river's verge where I get pure wine;
Grwst's Vale and the bank of Caer Awstin,
green valley of the gallons of wine;
three times worth the prince's kitchen,
the work turns heavily on his cook;
houses for wine, mead-temples,
a trestl and a trim buttery.
At once on all his wines
he has been head in every tongue.
Where would I go for saintly sessions?
To him and his fellow monks,
men numbered in Rome's people,
white and crimson are their gowns.
If his bosom and cope are white,
dressed thus he'll make a bishop,
and thus he'd go to conclave,
on trial to be Pope of Rome.
It's irksome work and folly
to strive for patronage.
They asked a thousand petty rents;
he asked for that of Maenan.
This man's support is like tree-bloom
over Meirionnydd's face.

Hyder Lewys Amhadawg
am erchi rhoi march yrhawg,
milwr rhwng Maelor a Rhos,
Tegaingl ei geraint agos,
a'i ddewis erbyn mis Mai
merch deg a march a'i dygai.
Trem hydd am gywydd a gais,
trwynbant yn troi'n ei unbais;
ffroen arth a chyffro'n ei ên,
ffrwyn a ddeil ei ffriw'n ddolen;
ffriw yn dal ffrwyn o daliwn,
a'i ffroen gau fal ffroen y gwn;
llygaid fal dwy ellygen
llymion byw'n llamu'n ei ben;
dwyglust feinion aflonydd,
dail saets wrth ei dâl y sydd;
trwsio fal goleuo glain
y bu wydrwr ei bedrain;
drythyll ar bedair wythoel,
gwreichionen o ben pob hoel;
ei flew fal sidan newydd
a'i rawn ar liw gwawn y gwŷdd,
sidan ym mhais ehedydd,
siamled yn hws am lwdn hydd.
Dylifo heb ddwylo'dd oedd,
neu weu sidan nes ydoedd.
Cnyw praffwasg yn cnoi priffordd,
cloch y ffair, ciliwch o'i ffordd.
Ei arial a ddyfalwn
i elain coch o flaen cŵn.
Nwyfawl iawn anifail oedd,
yn ei fryd nofio'r ydoedd.
Nid rhaid er peri neidio
rhoi dur fyth ar ei dor fo.
Dan farchog bywiog di-bŵl
ef a wyddiad ei feddwl;
llamu draw lle mwya drain,
llawn ergyd yn Llan Eurgain.
O gyrrir draw i'r gweirwellt

Lewis, son of Madoc, boldly
will now ask for a stallion.
He's a soldier between Maelor and Rhos,
and closely linked with Tegeingl.
He wishes to have, ready for May,
a pretty girl and a horse to carry her.
For a poem he seeks one with a stag's look,
a dimple-nosed one turning in his tunic,
a bear's nostril, a moving mouth,
a bridle holding his nose in a loop,
a nose which holds the bridle when we curb him,
the hollow nostril like the muzzle of a gun.
Eyes that are like two pears,
lively and keen, they leap from his head;
two slim and restless ears,
like sage leaves at his forehead;
like polishing of gems
was the glazier's dressing of his hooves;
brisk on four sets of eight nails,
with a spark from every nail's head.
His coat is like new silk,
his hair might be tree gossamer,
silk of a skylark's tunic
and camlet covering a young stag.
He spins without use of hands
and weaves a kerchief of silk.
Strong-waisted foal biting the highway,
the fair's alarm, out of his way!
His liveliness we liken
to a red fawn before the hounds.
He's such a lusty creature
that he floats to his purpose;
to make him prance you'll never
need to put steel to his belly;
under a brisk, keen horseman
he always knows his mind;
leaping over where thorns are greatest,
full of attack in Llan Eurgain.
If he's ridden over to the hayfield

ni thyr a'i garn wyth o'r gwellt.
Ystwyro cwrs y daran
a thuthio pan fynno'n fân;
bwrw naid i'r wybr a wnâi,
ar hyder yr ehedai.
Draw os gyrrwn dros gaered
gorwydd yr arglwydd a red;
dyrnfur yw'n dirwyn y fron,
deil i'r haul dalau'r hoelion.
Gwreichion a gair o honyn,
gwniwyd wyth bwyth ymhob un.
Sêr neu fellt ar sarn a fydd
ar godiad yr egwydydd;
ail y carw, olwg gorwyllt,
a'i draed yn gwau drwy dân gwyllt.
Neidiwr dros afon ydoedd,
naid yr iwrch rhag y neidr oedd.
Oes tâl am y sut elain
amgen na mawl am gnyw main?
Mae'n f'aros yma forwyn,
ferch deg, pe bai farch i'w dwyn.
Gorau 'rioed gair i redeg
march da i arwain merch deg.

he won't break eight stalks with his hoof.
Stirring to the thunder's course,
and mincingly stepping when he pleases,
he'd throw a leap at the sky,
he'd fly in confidence,
and if we ride him over a wall
this prince's horse will run on.
A battering ram winding up the hill,
he throws his nailheads to the sun;
sparks fly from every hoof,
eight points are pierced into each one;
there are stars or lightning on the road
at the lifting of his fetlocks.
Like a stag with fiercest gaze,
his feet weave through wild fire;
he jumps across a river
like a roebuck jumping from a snake.
Is there better payment for such a fawn
than praise of the slim beast?
There's a maiden, a beauty waiting for me,
if I had a horse to carry her off.
The best speed ever made was by
a good horse bearing a pretty girl.

35. Merch a'i Min fel y Mel

Melys pur weddus pereiddfin, gwn gael
  glyd afael gloi deufin;
gwen dlos a'i gwyndal iesin,
gloyw fêl yw 'mafel â'i min.

Fal y mel yw gafel ei gwefus beraidd,
  buraidd grair gariadus;
glana' bun ymhob ynys,
gwynna' groen dan y can grys.

Melys ei gwefus a'i gafael gan dant,
  hi a dentiai bob angel.
Pwy'n canu mwyn bynciau mêl?
Pwy'n well llais pennill isel?

35. To a Sweet-mouthed Girl

Sweet, pure, proper, sugared mouth, I know
    a snug grip for lip-locking.
  My pretty one of the shining brow,
  your lips are like clear honey.

Like honey the grip of her lip, sweet,
    pure, loving jewel,
  loveliest girl of all islands,
  whitest skin under flour-white shift.

Sweet is her lip and her grip with her teeth,
    she would tempt any angel.
  She is most sweetly vocal
  and best at the low harmony.

36. Hiraeth

Dos ymaith hiraeth orig o'm calon,
cilia i ffwrdd ychydig;
dywed i'm gwen felenfrig
fod dyn ac arno fyd dig.

36. Longing

Longing! leave my heart for an hour
    and turn away awhile
    to tell my yellow-topped girl
    that here's a man for whom the world is vile.

37. Tair Ewig o Sir Ddinbych

Fy nydd, fy newydd, fy nos, fy meddwl,
    fy maddau, 'rwyt agos;
minnau sydd wâr yn d'aros
ag od ei'n elyn im, dos.

Pob mwynder, ofer afiaith, pob meddwl,
    pob moddol gydymaith,
popeth, yn wir, ond hiraeth
yn gynnar iawn oddi genni'r aeth.

Mae afon a bron a brig y coedydd
    yn cadw tair ewig;
heddiw ni ŵyr bonheddig
na'u cael na phrofi mo'u cig.

Y bore byddant barod eu helynt
    am hela'r ewigod:
nid un a fynnem ni fod;
tair ohonyn' sydd hynod.

Nid â chŵn y mae i chwi eu hela,
    nid hwylus mo rheiny;
gorau it, fy nghâr, bwyntmannu
mewn coed heb illwng un ci.

37. Three Hinds of Denbighshire

My day, my news, my night, my mind,
    my forgiveness, you're near me
  and I am waiting meekly.
  Unless you'd be my foe, alight.

All joy, all empty jollity, all thought,
    all mannerly meeting,
  everything indeed but longing
  has suddenly gone away from me.

There's a river, a hillside and fresh boughs of trees
    that hide three hinds.
  Today no hunter finds
  them, or tries their willing flesh.

The morning you'll be ready, concerned
    with deer hunting:
  not one prey are we proposing,
  but a notable group of three.

Not with dogs should you decide to hunt us—
    that wouldn't be luckiest;
  better for you, my love, to tryst
  under trees with your dogs tied.

38. Englynion i'r Delyn

Dod fysedd eurwedd orig ar delyn
   rhag dolur a garwddig;
difyr ꝓedd maswedd miwsig
gwiwfael a dynn gofal dig.

Er caniad tynniad tannau ar fiwsig,
   er difesur bynciau,
dilyn fyth y delyn fau,
blith ydyw o blethiadau.

O ganiad cordiad cweirdant, a chrybwyll
   wych drebl a llorfdant,
lles o'i dwysgerdd llais desgant,
o'r llais e geir lles i gant.

38. Stanzas to the Harp

Set golden fingers for a moment to the harp,
    against hurt and displeasure;
  soft music's cheering measure
  most fittingly removes your torment.

For the plucked strings' melody, the music,
    the themes without number,
  I'll follow the harp for ever,
  for it is rich in tracery.

From the song of the tuned string, the hint
    of high treble and pipe chord,
  descanting to its grave concord
  the voice will bring us solacing.

39. Coed Marchan

Cywydd dros y gwiwerod a aeth i Lundain i ffilio ag i wneuthur affidafid ar y bil am dorri Coed Marchan yn ymyl Rhuthyn.

Blin ac afrydd yw'r gyfraith,
mae'n boen i'r gwiwerod bach;
mynd ar lawndaith i Lundain
â'u bloedd a'u mamaeth o'u blaen.
Gwych oedd hi'r wiwer goch hon,
dorllaes, yn medru darllen,
yn ymddiddan â'r cyngawr,
ac eto mae'n fater mawr.
Pan roed y Llyfr dan ei llaw
a choel oedd i'w chywilyddiaw,
hi ddywed wrth y beili,
'Sir Bribwm, un twym wyt ti!'
Ar ei llw hi ddywed fal hyn,
anrheithio holl goed Rhuthyn
a dwyn ei thŷ a'i sgubor
liw nos du, a'i chnau a'i stôr.
'Mae'r gwiwerod yn gweiddi
am y coed rhag ofn y ci.
Nid oes fry o goed y fron
ond lludw y derw llwydion.
Nid oes gepyll heb ei gipio,
na nyth brân byth i'n bro.
Mae'r tylluanod yn udo
am y coed, yn gyrru plant o'u co'.
Gwae'r dylluan rhag annwyd,
oer ei lle am geubren llwyd!
Gwae'r geifr am eu coed a'u cyll,
a pherchen hwch a pherchyll!
Gwae galon hwch folgoch hen
Dduw Sul am le i gael mesen!

39. Marchan Wood

A poem on behalf of the squirrels who went to London to file and make an affidavit on the bill for the cutting down of Marchan Wood, near Rhuthyn.

Odious and hard is the law
and painful to little squirrels.
They go the whole way to London
with their cry and their matron before them.
This red squirrel was splendid,
soft-bellied and able to read;
she conversed with the Council
and made a great matter of it.
When the Book was put under her hand
in the faith that this would shame her,
she spoke thus to the bailliff,
'Sir Bribem, you're a deep one!'
Then on her oath she said,
'All Rhuthyn's woods are ravaged;
my house and barn were taken
one dark night, and all my nuts.
The squirrels all are calling
for the trees; they fear the dog.
Up there remains of the hill wood
only grey ash of oak trees;
there's not a stump unstolen
nor a crow's nest left in our land.
The owls are always hooting
for trees; they send the children mad.
The poor owl catches cold,
left cold without her hollow trunk.
Woe to the goats, without trees or hazels,
and to the sow-keeper and piglets!
Pity an old red-bellied sow
on Sunday, in her search for an acorn.

163

Cadair y cathod coedion,
mi wn y tu llosgwyd hon.
Yn iach draenog; nac aerwy
na chafn moch ni cheir mwy.
Os rhostir gŵydd foel, rhaid fydd
â rhedyn Bwlch y Rhodwydd.
Crychias ni feirw crochan,
na breci mwy heb bricie mân.
O daw mawnen o'r mynydd
ar y glaw, oer a drud fydd.
Annwyd fydd yn lladd y forwyn,
oer ei thraed a defni o'i thrwyn.
Nid oes gay nac ysgyrren
na chae chwipio biach gul hen.
Gwir a ddywed Angharad,
oni cheir glo, yn iach i'n gwlad.'

The chair of the wild cats,
I know where that was burnt.
Goodbye hedgehog! No cow-collar
nor pig-trough will come from here any more.
If a plucked goose is to be roasted,
it must be with bracken from Rhodwydd Gap.
No pot will come to bubbling,
no beer will boil without small twigs;
and if peat comes from the mountain
in the rain, it's cold and dear.
Colds will exhaust the housemaid,
with cold feet and a dripping nose.
There's no hollow trunk or branch,
nor a fence for the beating of an old thin snipe.
Yes, Angharad spoke the truth,
if we don't get coal it's goodbye to our land.'

40. Coed Glyn Cynon

Aberdâr, Llanwnna i gyd,
plwy Merthyr hyd Lanfadon;
mwya adfyd a fu erioed
pan dorred Coed Glyn Cynon.

Torri llawer parlwr pur,
lle cyrchfa gwŷr a meibion;
yn oes dyddiau seren syw
mor arael yw Glyn Cynon.

O bai gŵr ar drafael dro
ac arno ffo rhag estron
fo gâi gan eos lety erioed
yn fforest Coed Glyn Cynon.

Llawer bedwen glas ei chlog
(ynghrog y byddo'r Saeson!)
sydd yn danllwyth mawr o dân
gan wŷr yr haearn duon.

Os am dorri a dwyn y bar,
llety yr adar gwylltion,
boed yr anras yn eu plith,
holl blant Alis ffeilsion!

Gwell y dylasai'r Saeson fod
ynghrog yng ngwaelod eigion,
uffern boen yn cadw eu plas
na thorri glas Glyn Cynon.

Clywais ddoedyd, ar fy llw,
fod haid o'r ceirw cochion
yn oer eu lle yn 'mado â'u plwy;
i ddu goed Mawddwy'r aethon.

40. Glyn Cynon Wood

Aberdare, Llanwynno through,
all Merthyr to Llanfabon;
there was never a more disastrous thing
than the cutting of Glyn Cynon.

They cut down many a parlour pure
where youth and manhood meet;
in those days of the regular star
Glyn Cynon's woods were sweet.

If a man in sudden plight
took to flight from foe,
for guest-house to the nightingale
in Cynon Vale he'd go.

Many a birch-tree green of cloak
(I'd like to choke the Saxon!)
is now a flaming heap of fire
where iron-workers blacken.

For cutting the branch and bearing away
the wild birds' habitation
may misfortune quickly reach
Rowenna's treacherous children!

Rather should the English be
strung up beneath the seas,
keeping painful house in hell
than felling Cynon's trees.

Upon my oath, I've heard it said
that a herd of the red deer
for Mawddwy's deep dark woods has left,
bereft of its warmth here.

Yn iach ymlid daear dwrch
na chodi iwrch o goedfron;
waitsio ewig, hi aeth yn f'oed
pan dorred coed Glyn Cynon.

O chas carw led ei droed
i'r coed o flaen cynyddon,
byth ni weler o'n rhoi tro
pan ddelo fo i Lyn Cynon.

Ac o delai ddeuliw'r can
i rodio glan yr afon,
teg oedd y lle i wneuthur oed
yn fforest Coed Glyn Cynon.

O daw'r arfer fel y bu gynt
o godi pynt ar afon,
caed eglwysi a gwŷdd tai,
fo'i ceir nhw'n llai yng Nglyn Cynon.

Mynna' i wneuthur arnynt gwest
o adar onest ddigon,
a'r dylluan dan ei nod
a fynna' i fod yn hangmon.

Ac o daw gofyn pwy a wnaeth
hyn o araith greulon,
dyn a fu gynt yn cadw oed
dan fforest Coed Glyn Cynon.

No more the badger's earth we'll sack
nor start a buck from the glade;
no more deer-stalking in my day,
now they've cut Glyn Cynon's shade.

If ever a stag got into a wood
with huntsmen a stride behind,
never again will he turn in his run
with Cynon Wood in mind.

If the flour-white girl once came
to walk along the brook,
Glyn Cynon's wood was always there
as a fair trysting nook.

If as in times gone by men plan
to span the mountain river;
though wood be found for house and church
Glyn Cynon's no provider.

I'd like to call on them a quest
of every honest bird,
where the owl, worthiest in the wood,
as hangman would be heard.

If there's a question who rehearsed
in verse this cruel tale,
it's one who many a tryst has kept
in the depth of Cynon Vale.

41. Cyhuddo a Barnu Cresyd

(Sinon, gwas Calcas, yn rhuthro i mewn at Briaf,
brenin Troya, a'i gyngor)

SINON *O rhyglydd bodd i'ch gras!*
Fe ffodd yr Arglwydd Calcas
yn ddisymwth neithiwr
i gymdeithas y Groegwyr.
Fy arglwyddi, rhaid gwylied
rhag eich twyllo trwy ymddiried.
Unferch ac anwylyd
i Galcas ydyw Cresyd;
nid ydyw'n cymryd ati
na'i cholled na'i ddrygioni.
Cyffelybrwydd y gwyddai
oddi wrth ei fynediad yntau.

PRIAF *Dos ymaith yn brysur,*
cyrch unferch y traetur
i gael cosbedigaeth. . . .
(PRIAF yn troi at ei feibon)
Oni edrychir, fy meibion,
i'r pethau hyn yn greulon
a'r tân parod a enynnodd
mewn amser i'w ddiffodd,
onide fe geir ymweled
ormod traeturied.
Rhaid gwneuthur yn helaeth
am hyn gosbedigaeth.
Onide 'rwyf yn ofni
y bydd gormod drygioni,
a Helenws a welir
yn doedyd y caswir.

(CRESYD yn dyfod gyda Sinon ac yn syrthio ar
ei gliniau)

170

41. The Trial of Cresyd

(Sinon, Calcas' servant, rushing in to Priaf, King of Troy, and his council)

SINON   All pleasure to your honour!
Lord Calcas has escaped
suddenly in the night
to the company of the Greeks.
My lords, you must guard yourselves
against deceit through trusting.
A dear and only daughter
is Cresyd to this Calcas,
but she won't take upon her
her loss or his iniquity.
It's likely that she knew
all about his departure.

PRIAF   Away you go quickly
and bring this traitor's daughter
to face her punishment.
(turning to his sons)
My sons, unless we see
cruelly to these things
and to this kindled fire
whilst it can be put out,
we shall be face to face
with much more treachery.
An ample punishment
must be inflicted for this,
otherwise I fear
a great increase of evil
and Helenus' forebodings
will turn to bitter truth.

(CRESYD comes in with SINON and falls upon her knees)

CRESYD   *Fy ngrasol arglwyddi,*
gyrasoch i'm cyrchu
mewn digofaint a digllondeb;
'rwy'n ofni gwrthwyneb.

PRIAF   *Ai tydi yw unferch Calcas,*
yr hen siwrl anghyweithas,
a werthai ei hollfraint
yn niwedd ei henaint
er bod yn dwyllodrus
i'w wlad anrhydeddus
a mynd mewn caethiwed
ymysg dieithriaid?
Dy gydwybod a'th arfer
sy'n cyhuddo dy ffalster;
ac euog wyt ti
o'i gwbl ddrygioni.
Am ei fawrddrwg a'i draha
ei genedl a ddinistria.
Arnat ti yn gyntaf,
Cresyd, y dechreuaf;
dy waed, dy einioes,
dy benyd, dy fawrloes,
a'th farwolaeth greulon
a esmwytha fy nghalon.
Beth a ddoedwch, f'arglwyddi,
pa farwolaeth a rown arni?

PARIS   *I'w llosgi hebryngwch*
am ei ffalster a'i diffaethwch;
a hynny yw marwolaeth.
Cyflawnwch y gyfraith!

ENEAS   *Perwch ei thaflu*
i bydew dyfnddu.
Rhy lân yw ei llosgi
am y fath ddrygioni.

ANTENOR *Bwriwch hi heno*

172

CRESYD My gracious lordships, you
    have caused me to be fetched
    in anger and displeasure.
    I fear adversity.

PRIAF Are you the only daughter
    of Calcas, uncivil churl,
    who would sell his honour
    at his old age's end
    in order to betray
    his renowned country
    by going to the captivity
    of strangers' company?
    Your conscience and your custom
    indict your falsity,
    for you are to be held guilty
    of all his wickedness.
    From his great wrong and treachery
    ruin may fall upon his land.
    Therefore with you first,
    Cresyd, will I begin.
    Your blood and your existence,
    your penance, your great pain
    and your most cruel death
    will tranquillize my heart.
    What do you say, my lords?
    What death shall we put on her?

PARIS Send her to be burnt
    for her false viciousness.
    Death, that is to say.
    See that the law's fulfilled!

ENEAS No, cause her to be thrown
    into a deep, dark pit.
    Burning is far too clean
    for such iniquity.

ANTENOR Let her be thrown tonight

at y llewod i'r ogo;
hi a ymborth am unpryd
y llewod newynllyd.

HELENWS   I garchardy gyrrwch
i ddwyn trymder a thristwch;
hyd einioes galaru
o fewn ei charchardy.

HECTOR   Hebryngwch i'r Groegwyr
ar ôl yr hen draetur.
Aed hon lle y mynned,
ni all hi fawr o niwed.

TROELUS   I'r gwirion na wnewch ddialedd
dros yr euog a'i gamwedd,
ac na fyddwch rhy greulon;
fe ddichon hon fod yn wirion.

CRESYD   Mau arglwyddi trugarog,
na fyddwch chwi rhy chwannog
i golli gwaed gwirionddall
dros ddrwg a beiau arall.
O gwnaeth Calcas i chwi benyd,
difalais ydoedd Cresyd;
efô mewn euog ateb
a minnau mewn gwiriondeb;
y tad yn gweuthud camwedd
a'r ferch yn dwyn dialedd.
Dyna gyfraith rhy atgas,
ymhell yn erbyn eich urddas!
Pe gwnaethai fi'n gydnabyddus
â'i ddichell frad twyllodrus,
ni fuaswn i mewn gafael
yn aros ymysg rhyfel,
na rhyfelwyr yn tramwy
cyn fynyched lle y byddwy,
a minnau'n unig forwyn.
Ni ddichon merch ond achwyn.

into the lions' cave;
at least she'd make one meal
for those hungry beasts.

HELENUS Put her in a prison-house
to suffer gloom and sadness,
to waste her life away,
grieving within her prison.

HECTOR Send her off to the Greeks
after the old traitor!
Wherever this girl goes
she'll do but little harm.

TROELUS On the innocent take no vengeance
for the misdeed of the guilty.
And don't be over cruel;
she may be innocent.

CRESYD Oh, my gracious lords,
don't set your hearts so much
on spilling innocent blood
for another's evil deeds.
If Calcas caused you pain,
Cresyd was without malice.
His is the guilty answer
and mine is innocence.
The father culpable
and the daughter punished,
that's a detestable law
and much against your honour.
If he had made me party
to his treacherous defection,
I should not be within reach,
lingering amidst a war,
with soldiers passing by
frequently where I am,
and I a lonely maiden.
A girl can only lament!

Ef a wyddai, fy arglwyddi,
na allai ymddiried imi,
a hynny a barodd iddo
mor ddisymwth ymado.
Gwae fi na fyddai f'einioes,
er dioddef nych a mawrloes,
yn iawn abl i ddiwygio
yr uthr weithred honno;
ac na liwid, er aros,
i un o'm cenedl mo'r achos.
Fy arglwyddi, ni ddymunwn
i chwi'r awron mo'm pardwn.
(TROELUS yn dywedyd yn isel yng nghlust ei
frawd HECTOR)

TROELUS Hector, fy annwyl frawd,
amddiffynnwr gwiriondlawd,
erfyn yr wyf i'ch mawredd
amddiffyn gwirionedd.
Amddiffynnwch chwi Gresyd,
ei heinioes a'i bywyd.

HECTOR Elusen i chwi wrando
ar ruddfanus wylo
a thrugarhau wrth achwyn
y wirionaidd forwyn.
Pe buasai'n gydnabyddus
â'i fynediad twyllodrus,
dyledus naturiol
gadw'n gyfrinachol
y pethau, drwy fawrloes,
a gollai i'w thad ei einioes.
Os byddir mor greulon,
beth a ddywed y gelynion?
'Lle bo'r fath greulondeb,
ni all fod gwroldeb.'

TROELUS (ac ar hyn mae'n syrthio mewn cariad)
Rho fy einioes drosti
o bu yn hon ddrygioni,

176

My lords, he knew he couldn't
put his trust in me
and that's the reason why
he fled so suddenly.
My wish is that my life,
by suffering want and pain,
could fully compensate
for this most terrible deed,
that this cause might not be
a shame upon my nation.
Then, lords, I'd not be begging
you now to give me pardon.
(TROELUS *whispers in his brother* HECTOR'S *ear*)

TROELUS   Hector, my dear brother,
defender of poor innocence,
I call upon your greatness
here to defend the truth.
Be a defence for Cresyd,
the saving of her life.

HECTOR   I beg of you to listen
to this pitiful weeping
and to take mercy on
this innocent girl's complaint.
If she had been made party
to his treacherous going,
it would be natural
for her to keep it secret,
for this most terrible thing
would cost her father's life.
If you behave thus cruelly
what will our enemies say?
'Where there's such cruelty
there can't be bravery.'

TROELUS   (*and now he falls in love*)
I will pledge my life
that there's no evil in her,

nac erioed ymarfer
â thwyll neu ffalster.
Yr ydym yn atolwg i chwi
roi maddeuant iddi;
ac o'r awr hon allan
'rwyf i Troelus fy hunan
yn caethiwo fy rhyddid
dros gywirdeb Cresyd.
(TROELUS yn troi at SINON, yr hwn a'i cyhuddasai
    hi, ac yn dywedyd wrtho yn isel)

Tydi fydredd celwyddog,
i bob achwyn yn chwannog,
dy rodresus ddyfeisiau
ydyw arwain celwyddau
a bwrw beiau ar wirion
trwy faleisus ddychmygion,
ac esgusodi camwedd
ac anafus fuchedd
er mwyn ysgwyd dy gynffon
ar bob math ar ddynion.
Onibai fod yn bresennol
fy ngwir dad naturiol,
myn yr holl dduwiau
rhown drwyddot fy nghleddau!

PRIAF   *Eich dymuniant nis gwrthneba*
dros golli tir yr Asia.
Cewch Gresyd yn wirion
a diolchwch i'm meibion.
Awn i mewn i fyfyr
beth sydd ychwaneg i wneuthur.

HECTOR   *(wrth Gresyd wedi i'r lleill ymado)*
I'ch cartref hwnt cerddwch,
trymder mawr na ddygwch.
Cymrwch eich rhyddid
yn llawen, a'ch bywyd,
ac am gymaint ag y gallaf
rhowch eich hyder arnaf.

178

nor ever any practice
of treachery or deceit.
We now petition you
to be forgiving to her
and henceforth, from this hour
will I, Troelus, myself
pledge all my liberty
for Cresyd's honesty.
(TROELUS *turns to* SINON *who had accused her,*
    whispering)
You lying rottenness,
eager for all informing,
your swaggering device
is to lead lies around
and put the blame on innocence
with your imagined malice
and to excuse the evil
of your own blemished living
by shaking of your tail
on every kind of person.
Were it not for the presence
of my true natural father,
by all the gods that are
I'd put my sword through you!

PRIAF Your plea is not opposed
even though Asia be lost.
Go, Cresyd, in innocence
and give thanks to my sons.
Let us go in to meditate
on what is more to do.

HECTOR (*to* CRESYD *when the others have left*)
Go back now to your home
and leave all heaviness.
Take up your liberty
happily, and your life.
And put your trust in me
to the utmost of my power.

42. O Blaid Y Gwragedd

Gwrandawed yr holl bobloedd
o'r meysydd a'r mynyddoedd,
lle y gwnaed gogan ar goedd
i'r merched a'r gwrageddoedd
am ddryced eu 'marweddiad
yn nechreuad yr oesoedd.

Wrth edrych a mynegi
pob llyfrau ac ystori,
ni aned i gydoesi
un heb bechod i'w henwi.
Pawb sy'n haeddu dialedd
ond trugaredd Dduw Celi.

O flaen barnu, darllenan
yr wythfed bennod o Ifan,
lle dywed Duw yn fuan
wrth y bobloedd a ddoethan
â gwraig ato'n pechu'n drist
yn erbyn Crist ei hunan;

Wrthynt Iesu a ddyfod,
'Hwn ohonoch sy heb bechod,
coded garreg, rhoed ddyrnod;
ei llabyddio sydd amod.'
Ac euog oedd yr holl wlad,
a Duw y Tad yn gwybod.

Wrth y wraig doedai yn dyner,
'Dos ymaith drwy ffyddlonder;
o bechod nac ymarfer.'
Ac erchi i'r ynifer
na roed neb farn ddiddoeth
achos na ddoeth mo'r amser.

42. *In Defence of Woman*

Let all the nations listen
from the meadows and the mountains
where a satire was made public
against girls and women
for the ill of their behaving
in the beginning of ages.

If you contemplate and render
all books and every story,
not one was born in any age
to be named without her sin;
they merit justice, there's no doubt,
without God's heavenly mercy.

But before judging let all read
the eighth chapter of John,
where God quickly said to those
that brought a woman to him,
who most sadly had transgressed
against Christ himself;

to them Jesus said, 'Let
him of you who is without sin
raise a stone and fist
to kill by covenant.'
The whole land was guilty rather
and God the Father knew it.

To the woman he said softly,
'Go thou in faithfulness
and use no sin hereafter.'
To the multitude his charge was,
none should rashly make judgement,
that moment had not come.

Efa li wiodd i Efa
ei phechod a'i thraheustra;
o hon y daeth Maria
i ddiwygio hynyma,
a'i Mab tynnodd o'r ffwrn gaeth
holl hiliogaeth Adda.

Joachim tad Mair ydoedd,
ac Anna ei mam a hanoedd
o hen waed y brenhinoedd,
o lwyth Siwda a'i cenhedloedd,
o gyff Dafydd, broffwyd Crist;
nid ydyw trist yr achoedd.

Pan oedd Mair dair o flwyddau
yng Nghaersalem ddiamau
y'i cysegrwyd yn ddiau
i Dduw ei hun a'i wyrthiau
ac ohoni yr addewid
y genid y gŵr gorau.

Morwyn cyn cael Crist helaeth
ac, yn feichiog, morwyn odiaeth,
morwyn ar ei enedigaeth,
morwyn wedi yn famaeth;
a Iesu ei mab ar bren heb drai
a brynai'r holl genhedlaeth.

Pum rhinwedd a rôi'r Drindod
i ferch rhagor gwr parod;
wedi hynny fe ddyfod,
ac iawn i bawb gydnabod
y llanwai hil y wraig wâr
nef a daear hynod.

Y rhinwedd gynta'n gymwys
oedd creu merch ym Mharadwys
a honno oedd bur a chymwys
a'r glana a fu mewn eglwys;

He reprimanded Eve
for her sin and arrogance,
and from her came Mary
to make recompense,
whose son from the closed furnace
drew all the race of Adam.

Joachim was her father
and Anna, her mother, came
from the old blood of kings,
from the generation of Judah,
from stem of David, prophet of Christ,
a list far from unhappy.

When Mary was three years old
and in Jerusalem
she was made consecrate
to God and his strange works,
that from her by foretelling
might spring the best of men.

Virgin before the gift of Christ
and, pregnant, a rare virgin,
a virgin at his birth
and a virgin suckling him.
Jesus her son upon the tree
paid the fee for man.

Five virtues the Trinity gave
to maids but not to men.
With that in mind it's proper
that we should all acknowledge
gentle woman's progeny
as filling sky and earth.

The first virtue was to create
a girl in paradise,
and she was pure and proper,
as pretty as ever went to church,

yno ni chreir yr un byth
o'r gwehelyth gwiwlwys.

Yr ail rinwedd oedd fynnu
o Grist yr Arglwydd Iesu
(y gŵr a fynnai'n prynu
ac ef a ddaw i farnu)
ei eni'n fab o gnawd merch
yr oedd a'i serch i'w charu.

Y drydedd rhinwedd nefol—
i ferch yn fyw gorfforol
ynddangoses Duw grasol
yn ei wir gnawd daearol
wedi ei godi o'i fedd dan faen
o flaen y deuddeg 'postol.

Pedwerydd rhinwedd helaeth—
dwyn merch yn ei chorffolaeth
a'i rhoi'n y nef, medd gwybodaeth,
dan Dduw yn ben cenhedlaeth,
lle nid âi ond Duw a'r Gair
a'r hon Fair ei famaeth.

Y bumed rhinwedd enwog—
gael o Elen luyddog
y groes fendigaid wyrthiog
(hon nis câi filwr arfog)
ac adnabod o'r tair croes
wirgroes Duw drugarog.

Mair Fadlen, pawb a'i gwybu,
er ei bod yn gordderchu
yr ydoedd Duw'n ei charu;
hi a beidiodd drwy 'difaru
ac â'i gwallt a'i dagrau y'i caed
yn sychu traed yr Iesu.

Sant Catrin y ferch rasol

but of her sweet tribe not one
will there again be born.

The second virtue was that Christ,
our Lord Jesus and the man
who was intent to save us
and will come to judge us,
should choose birth from a girl's flesh,
whose every wish was loving.

The third heavenly virtue—
to a woman in living flesh
the gracious God appeared
in his true earthly body,
having risen from his stone-capped grave
before the twelve apostles.

The fourth bountiful virtue,
the taking of a physical woman,
her placing in heaven, says wisdom,
under God the chief of peoples.
Where only God and the Word were
this Mary went as Mother.

The fifth famous virtue—
that the retinued Helena
got the blessed miraculous cross
(denied to the armed soldier)
and knew from the three crosses
the true cross of the merciful God.

Mary Magdalen we all know;
though she lived a wanton
yet did God still love her.
She changed through her repentance
and tearfully with her hair
dried the bare feet of Jesus.

Saint Catherine the gracious

a fu er mwyn Crist nefol
ar y rhod ddur afrifol
lle y claddwyd ei chorff dwyfol.
O'i dwy fron y caed yn frau
y ddau olew fydol.

Sant Marged wrth weddïau,
wedi i'r ddraig ei llyncu hithau,
hi a dyfodd yn ei genau
onid aeth y ddraig yn ddrylliau
ac a ddaeth hon wrth ei bodd,
y modd y buasai orau.

Caradog oedd ŵr creulon;
am na châi ef Wenfrewi dirion,
torri ei phen, lle y caed ffynnon,
a thrwy nerth Iesu gyfion
Beuno a roes arni ei phen
a byw fu wen ac union.

Ni dderfydd im fynegi
faint o ferched, na'u henwi,
a ddewisodd Dduw Celi
yn santesau ei oleuni
i ymoddef gynt er ei fwyn
gur heb gŵyn, a'u poeni.

Gwraig Eliwed mirain dirion
gwnaeth foliant miwsig cyson
i Dduw, prynwr Cristnogion,
dros foddi Pharo greulon;
ac yhi oedd wen a chlaer
ac oedd chwaer i Aaron.

Pan oedd Dafydd broffwyd cu
gan henaint yn gwanychu,
Abisag oedd i'w ymgleddu
cylch saith mlynedd ar untu,
ac i'w wely main ei hael,

for heavenly Jesus' sake
went on the monstrous wheel of steel;
her godly body was broken
and from her breast so frail
came the two oils of the world.

Saint Margaret through prayer,
when the dragon swallowed her,
grew within its jaws
and thus split the dragon.
She came out happily,
in the most seemly fashion.

Caradoc turned to cruelty
when he failed to have Gwenfrewi,
cut off her head and straight there sprang
a well of water, through Christ's might.
Beuno put back her head on her,
upright and fair she lived.

I could never convey
nor name how many girls
the God of Heaven has chosen
to be his saints of light
and to suffer for his sake
pain and ache patiently.

Eliwed's fair and gentle wife
made praise in constant music
for God, redeemer of Christians,
to drown the cruel Pharaoh;
she was shining and fair
and she was Aaron's sister.

When the good prophet David
was weakening in old age,
Abisag was comfort to him
the circuit of seven years in one place
and the slim-browed girl in his bed

heb na'i chael na'i llygru.

Pan oedd Johoas wirion
a Jonathan gŵr union
yn ffoi rhag eu gelynion,
mewn basged yn y ffynnon
Sehosaba, gwraig dda ei modd,
a achubodd y dynion.

Sara ferch Rachel addwyn,
wrth arch ei thad a'i dolwyn,
a briodai rhag achwyn
ŵr i gadw'r gyfraith drylwyn
a'i gydfod i'w hoes yn gu
a marw a fu yn forwyn.

Rebeca, gwraig ddigyffro,
oedd gyfiawn yn ymordrio,
wedi ei marw ei chuddio;
rhag daed oedd ei gortho,
Pedr a gâi gan Dduw a'n clyw
ei chodi'n fyw i rodio.

Wedi marw Lasar obry
yn y ddaear a'i gladdu
a bod tridiau ar untu
a'i gorff yn dechrau llygru,
câi Fartha ei chwaer gan Dduw tri
yn fyw ei godi i fyny.

Sara a Rachel oedd gyfion
am na phlanten' yn bruddion
i amlhau cenedl ddynion,
a ddygant eu morynion
at eu gwŷr, nid i'w twyllo
ond i geisio etifeddion.

Pan oedd y proffwyd Dafydd
a'i fab Absolom beunydd

was not enjoyed or sullied.

When the innocent Jonas
and the honest Jonathan
were in flight from enemies,
with a basket down a well
Jehosaba, the well-mannered wife,
saved the life of both.

Meek Sarah, daughter of Rachel,
lamenting at her father's bier,
forestalled complaint by marrying
a man to please the vigilant law.
She lived his life out at his side
and she died a virgin.

Rebecca, tranquil lady,
was right in ordering
a covering for her after death,
but though her canopy was good
the listening God chose Peter
to bring her back to walk.

When Lazarus died over there
and was buried in earth
and had been three days in the place,
his flesh beginning to decay,
his sister Martha sought the triple God
to raise his body to life.

Sarah and Rachel were right
not to bear children sadly
to multiply man's race;
they took their handmaidens
to their men, not in deceit
but to get them heirs.

When the prophet David
and Absolom his son each day

yn taro ar ei gilydd
heb gymodi i'r gwledydd,
Esther oedd wraig dda ei 'madrodd
a'u cymododd yn llonydd.

Pan fu'r wybr, pawb a'i clywodd,
wedi ei chau rhag glaw yn ormodd,
Eleias, broffwyd iawnfodd,
drwy gyngor gwraig gweddiodd
i ardymeru y byd draw:
gwlith a glaw a gafodd.

Pan oedd wŷr fry'n troi cwysau
ar ol erydr a thidau
heb orffwys na chwarae
yn poeni eu traed a'u breichiau,
dyfeisiodd San Ffraid leian
chwelydr harddlan eu moddau.

Pan oedd y bobl yn noethion,
heb ddim dillad ar ddynion,
Palathas, gwraig oedd gyfion,
a ddyfeisiodd yn union
o eilio gwlân a'i nyddu i wlad
i gael dillad ddigon.

Pan oedd y byd wrth ddechrau,
heb na gerddi na llysiau,
Seres, gwraig o'r rhyw gorau
a ddyfeisiodd bob hadau
i drwsio bwyd yn ddiwael
ac i gael aroglau.

Merch a'i henw Nicostrata
oedd o lwyth Seth ap Adda;
o'i hathrylith yn fwya'
ac o rad Duw gorucha'
a ddyfeisiodd mewn moddau
lythrennau Lladin gynta.

struck against each other,
with no concord in the land,
Esther was the good wife whose talk
brought them to walk in peace.

When the firmament (we've all heard it)
was shut against the rain,
Elias the righteous prophet
prayed by counsel of a wife
to temper the world through
and he got dew and rain.

When men of old turned furrows
behind the plough and the chain,
without rest or play
torturing their feet and arms,
Saint Brigid the sweet sister
made seed-spreaders for them.

When the nations were naked
and men wore no clothes,
Palathas the good wife
rapidly invented
a means to spin and weave the wool
till all were fully clothed.

And when the world began
with no herbs or gardens,
Ceres, the best sort of wife,
invented every seed
to garnish the fine food
and give it a good flavour.

A girl called Nicostrata,
of the tribe of Seth and Adam,
out of her greatest learning,
and God's highest grace
devised the origin
of the first Latin letters.

Merch a'i henw Eisys wenbryd,
a hon oedd ddoeth i'w bywyd
a chraff ymhob celfyddyd
a mawr ei chyfarwyddyd,
a ddyfeisiodd mewn lluniau
lythrennau Edsipt hefyd.

Naw Sibyl, dyna'u henwau,
a wnaethont naw llyfr golau,
a daeth un o'r merchedau
at frenin Rhufain gaerau
a gofyn trychan talen
o aur hen am y llyfrau.

A'r brenin a'i gwrthododd
achos y pris oedd ormodd;
tri o'r llyfrau a losgodd
yn ei dig, pan nas cafodd,
a cheisio yr un pris yn drech
am y chwech adawodd.

A'r brenin a'i gwrthodai:
hon eilwaith tri a losgai
o ddig wrtho nas rhoddai
achos y boen a gawsai,
a cheisio yr un pris yn fri
am y tri adawsai.

Gorfu i'r brenin, oedd dynnaf
pan aethpwyd i'r fan eithaf,
am na fedrai'r cais cyntaf,
gymryd y fargen decaf:
rhoi pris y naw drwy fawr gri
am y tri diwethaf.

Ac fe wyddys bod felly
a hyd ddydd farn y pery
a oedd yn Rhufain obry
i waered ac i fyny,

A fair-faced girl called Isis,
a wise one in her living
and sharp in every art
and a great story-teller—
she devised in pictures
the characters of Egypt.

And then there were nine Sibyls,
who made the nine bright books.
One of these girls once came
to the king of the towers of Rome
and asked three hundred talents
of old gold in payment for them.

But the king refused:
the price was far too high.
So she burnt three books
in spite at his refusal
and asked in a firm voice
the same price for the six.

Once more the king refused
and once more three were burnt
in anger at his slowness
and the pain it caused her.
She asked the price, with dignity,
for the three still left.

And so the stubborn king,
(it went to this extreme)
because he failed at the first chance
to take the best of bargains,
with a great cry gave the price of nine
to gain the three remaining.

It is well known that thus
and till the Judgement Day
these books remained in Rome above,
and up and down the country

a chyfrwyddyd i'r holl wlad
a gaed o'r llyfrau hynny.

Iawn i bawb ganmol Cambria
a dwyn cof cyfraith Farsia;
merch onest oedd Siwsana,
a mawr oedd clod Rebeca
a Semiramys ruddwin,
gwraig i frenin Siria.

Merch sy deca'n y nefoedd
ond Duw, brenin niferoedd;
ar y ddaear a'r moroedd
ar a aned o'r holl fobloedd
merch sy decaf ei blodau
a gorau ei gweithredoedd.

Llawn yw merch o rinweddau
a chwrtais ymhob moddau
ac arafaidd ei geiriau
a synhwyrol ei champau
a phob amser yn ei phwyll
megis cannwyll olau.

Gwraig sy lon a bonheddig,
fal gwenynen o'r goedwig
hi a wna lawer o 'chydig;
hi a geidw'i gŵr yn ddiddig;
i wneuthur oed tan y rhiw,
nid ydyw wiw mo'i chynnig!

Pe cawn einioes ac iechyd
fal Moesen a Noe hefyd
a chanu awr ac ennyd
nos a dydd heb seguryd,
ni dderfyddai im o'm serch
ganmol merch a'i glendid.

Pe byw hwn a'i oferedd

knowledge and skill to the whole land
was handed from these books.

Justly we praise Cambria
and learn the laws of Marsia:
an honest girl was Susanna,
praiseworthy was Rebecca
and the white-cheeked Semiramis,
the wife of Syria's king.

A woman is fairest in heaven
after the God of Hosts,
on earth and on the seas,
and of all people born
a girl is of flowers the fairest
and noblest in her deeds.

A girl is full of virtues,
in every way she's courteous,
her speech is ever gentle,
her manners sensible,
and prudence in her burns as bright
as in a lighted candle.

A woman is merry and noble
and, like a bee of the woods,
she will make much from little.
She'll keep her husband happy
and as for trysting under the hill,
you'll fare ill if you offer.

If I lived long and healthily
like Moses and like Noah
and wrote never-endingly
each day without idleness,
my love would never let me cease
from praise of woman's beauty.

If he still lived in vanity

a wnaeth yr araith chwerwedd
heb synnwyr nac amynedd
na mesur na chynghanedd,
mi a wnawn iddo gnoi ei dafod
am a ddyfod ar wragedd.

O bydd neb a chwenycho
yn y mater ymbledio,
ymddangosed heb risio
a dweded pwy a fyddo;
e gaiff ateb digon croch
ac och i'r cynta a gilio!

O daw gofyn a gwiriaw
yn uchel ac yn ddistaw
pwy a wnâi yr araith hylaw
ar draethodl a'i myfyriaw,
Wiliam Cynwal, ac nis gwad
pan fyddo'r wlad yn gwrandaw.

who made that bitter satire
without good sense or patience,
without metre or concord of sound,
I'd make him bite his tongue
for the wrong he spoke of women.

If anyone should desire
to plead upon this cause,
let him quietly arise
and say who he is;
he'll get a forceful answer,
the yielder shall cry 'Oh!'

If it is asked and verified
aloud or secretly
who made this fit oration
and rhymed this meditation,
William Cynwal won't deny it
though you cry it through the land.

43. Heldrin ar y Môr

Dylynais diwael enyd
y dŵr i Spaen ar draws byd
tybio ond mudo i'r môr
y trowswn wrth bob trysor
Rodio a dilio y dŵr
reudus a fydd pob rodiwr
Prynais long prinheis y wlad
am arian ir kymeriad
futliais hon burion yn ber
futlio lle i roedd aml fwtler
heliais wyr anhwylus waith
i foriaw llwyr oferwaith
iddewon liw duon dig
uffernawl foliau ffyrnig
mynd ir llong i mendio'r llu
at angen dechrau tyngu
ag ar y bwrdd dragwrdd draw
y meistr yn kael i mwystriaw
Tyrn kapstro ag udo gwers
way ankar ol yw iwnkers
ymorol whear is meirick
klowch barabl kwyl the kabl kwik
saer diboen siwr yw deubott
Say the pwmp yw si the pott
tro i falltan trwy felltith
trum the shipp chwipp yn ddi chwith
brysia yna brys anwr
bring in the bowling you bwr
Bear hard yp i gael bwrw haint
Bear alwff be bwrw lyffaint
yw bwni ffast the boned
sownd ffein with the lein and led
veer the seith labi methiant
abowt agayn bettau gant

43. A Poem to show the Trouble that befell him when
he was at Sea.

I followed, o splendid season,
the water over the world to Spain,
thinking that, taking to the sea,
I should come by all treasure.
Wandering, sieving the waters
needily, is the seaman's fate.
I bought a ship, stripped the land
for money for the venture;
victualled it fitly and fair,
victualled where butlers abounded.
I gathered men, a gloomy task,
for utterly vain sea-faring,
some vicious dark-hued Jews,
hell-bellied and abusive.
I took ship to train the men,
then came the need for cursing.
There was a roaring on board,
the master calling muster.
'Turn the capstan,' he howled an order,
'Weigh anchor, all you younkers!'
A question, 'Where is Meyrick?'
Then the words, 'Coil the cable quick!'
Deubott the carpenter's diligent,
'Try the pump, you see to the pit.'
'Turn you to fire and be damned!'
'Trim the ship, whip to it, yare!
Make haste there, haste, you waster!
Bring in the bowline, you boor!
Bear hard up to throw off plague;
bear aloof if it rain toads!
You, Bunny, make fast the bonnet,
sound fine with the line and lead.
Veer the sheet, impotent booby;
about again, if a hundred times!'

ffarwel Eingland ar sand sych
a seeli ynys haelwych
rowl away with reiol wings
i barlio dua'r bwrlings
Hears Atkins whear is wotkok
Bear al neight reight to the rok
gwila yna gael anap
owr kwrs is the sythr kap
tak haight yn llwyr synwhurol
thow poyns yonder is the pol
today dal mewn teidiau du
i feering ni awn y foru
a hwling loos the haliard
yn brysur iawn brysia ir yard
bring ner the tymber tomboy
what sheer a kan of beer boy
mwmson hoes up the maensael
Be meeri I see a sael
gif sias er a gefais i
owt topsael yw lowt tipsi
gif way ar y gauafwynt
kynill ag ynill y gwynt
ystarbwrd larbwrd lwyrboen
klir a bafft kilia or boen
port hard the helm fastardyn
ystydi thws dydi ddyn
keep the preis lwk owt weisli
hear thow lad ynder thy li
siwt a pis wrth gomisiwn
saethodd dri y hi yn lle hwn
siwt agayn brod seid gyner
will be braf iff we haf her
ffeight ffor stor and lef sorow
ffear not shiwt the weild ffeir now
lay her a bwrd er dwrdiaw
now enter drwy fenter draw

Farewell England and dry sand
and Scilly, lovely island.
Roll away with royal wings
to parley off the Burlings.

'Here's Atkins. Where is Woodcock?
Bear all night right to the Rock.
Beware of any mishap;
our course is the southern cape.
Take height in all good sense.
Thou Poyns, yonder is the Pole.'

To-day we hold in dark tides,
we'll veer away tomorrow.
'You, Hulling, loose the haliard!
Off you go along the yard!
Bring near the timber, tomboy!
What cheer? A can of beer, boy!
Munson, hoist up the mainsail.
Be merry, I see a sail.
Give chase, for all I've got!
Out topsail, you tipsy lout!
Give way!' In the winter storm
we mustered and mastered the wind,
starboard and larboard labouring.
'Clear abaft, keep clear of trouble!
Port the held hard, you bastard!
Steady thus, man! Do you hear?
Keep the prize (look out wisely,
hear thou, lad) under thy lee.
Now fire a piece in order.'
Instead, he shot three into her.
'Fire another broadside, gunner!
We'll be brave if we have her.
Fight for store and leave sorrow,
fear not, shoot the wild fire now!
Lay her aboard!' In all the din,
'Now enter, venture over!'

Ag wrth ymladd gwarth amlwg
wee lost owr ar lestr a mwg
gif bak lest al be taken
oes modd ffor to saf sym men
we twk wnffortunat day
wee ffeynd wee meynd this mynday
krio iownlef kur anlwk
o lord hear is to hard lwk
ffowk kari labi libin
is drownd pan oedd wres y drin
Brown Robin awstin withal
is dead and so is dwdal
wenfford Rowland and winffild
wiliam and kobam is kild
Tom Meirik dik boda dyn
is hyrt and so is hortyn
owr shipp is wrth ymgrippio
weak and ffwl of leak bi lo
o daw atom bydd dottiad
storm we are in tw hard stad
gwttw o hirboen gett harbowr
baris yw the beer is sowr
hyn a gefais hun gofal
am y daith yma a dal
Dowt yma o daw Tomas
adre yn siwr or gloewddwr glas
bee ffor I will pil or part
bei a shipp Il bee shepart.

Whilst fighting, open discredit,
we lost our men on the vessel in smoke.
'Give back, lest all be taken!
Is there a means to save some men?'
We took an unfortunate day,
we find this Monday,
loudly bewailing fortune's blow,
'O Lord, here is too hard luck!'
Foulk Harry, awkward booby,
is drowned in the battle's din;
Brown Robin Austin withal
is dead, and so is Duddal.
Wenford, Rowland and Winfield,
William and Cobham are killed.
Tom, Meyrick, Dick, each one
is hurt, and so is Horton.
Our ship in grappling so
is weak and full of leak below,
and if a storm now takes us
we'll be in too hard a state.
'Go to, pain; let's get to port!
Barris, the beer is sour.'

Thus I got a sleep of care
in payment for this venture.
I doubt if Thomas from here
will get home safe from the green sea.
Before I will pillage or part
by ship, I'll be a shepherd.

44. I Merch Lân

Cerais wiwferch, cwrs ufudd,
a'r dagrau oll 'rhyd y grudd.
Os tlws oedd Fenws feinwedd
a gloyw'n wir â glân wedd,
tlysach a gloywach mewn gwlad,
er fy nghur, yw fy nghariad.
Os glân ydoedd ychwaneg
Minerfa, Deiana deg,
dau lanach ydyw 'leni
yng nghwr dail fy nghariad i.
Os hardd oedd Balas hirddoeth
a Dsuwno neu Ddeido ddoeth,
harddach, pereiddiach yw pryd
y fun olau, f'anwylyd.
Os iraidd fynwes arian
Medea, Luwcresia lân,
ireiddiach, hoywach yw hon,
gwawr gulael a'm gwir galon.
Os teg a fu Gresyd wen
a thyner iawn ei thonnen,
tegach, heb ddim taeogedd,
fy meistres gynnes ei gwedd.
Os gwen fu Elen ennyd
a glân o beth glain y byd,
dau wynnach ydyw wyneb
fy nghariad, yn anad neb.
Diolched gwen feinwen fau
ei glaned ar ei gliniau.

44. *To a Pretty Girl*

I loved a girl, way of obedience,
and there were tears down my cheeks.
If slim-shaped Venus was fair,
truly bright and lovely of face,
fairer and brighter in all the land
is my love, in spite of my wound.
And if Minerva was fair,
or sweet Diana for that matter,
doubly fair in this year
is my love in a corner of leaves.
If long-wisdomed Pallas was splendid,
or Juno, or wise Dido,
sweeter and more splendid the face
of the bright girl who is my love.
If fresh was the silver breast
of Medea or lovely Lucretia,
this one is fairer and trimmer,
my fine-browed one and my true heart.
If lovely Cressid was fair,
with a skin of great tenderness,
tenderer, yet quite unrustic,
is my warm-featured mistress.
If Helen once was fair,
and a fair thing is the jewel of the world,
twice whiter is the face
of my love, above all girls.
Let my pretty one give thanks
upon her knees that she's so beautiful.

45. Y Llamhidydd

Y llamhidydd llym hoywdeg
yn llamu'n frau tonnau teg,
llo gweilgi, lliwiog ael gerth,
llyfna gwrs fab llefain gerth.
Llawen ydwyt lle'i nodir,
llon ym mrig ton ym mro tir;
ffrom olwg, ffriw ymyloer,
a phryd arth yn y ffrwd oer.
Crychneidia, cryna fel cryd,
cyhwfan acw hefyd.
Ymdrech â dwfr, madarch du,
edrych arno a chwyrnu.
Yr ydwyt yn aredig
y tonnau brau yn eu brig,
y môr hallt yma a hollti,
eigion y don a fyn di.
Ysgod glew yw'r esgud glân,
ysgwl môr, ysgil marian;
gwiber dwfr ymgeibia'r don,
golwg a ofna galon.
Torwyn wyd, tirion odiaeth,
tramwywr y cefnddwr caeth;
twrch heli, taer uchelwaith,
treigla'r môr, tro eglur maith.
Drwy yr haf pan dry yr hin
doi i rocio ymlaen drycin.
Baedd ffyrnig, buddai uffernwyllt,
blin a llawn gwanc blaen llanw gwyllt;
paladr a'i frestplat aur frig,
pysgodyn pais gauedig;
llwyth dyfroedd, llyweth dwyfron,
llithra a dal 'rhyd llethr y don.
Cyfrwy dŵr, cyfeiria di,
cyrch helynt i'r croch heli,

45. The Porpoise

Porpoise, swift, trim and handsome,
finely leaping the fair waves,
colourful, sharp-browed sea-calf,
make smooth the course of one who weeps.
You are happy when you can be seen,
merry in the wave-top where land ends.
Of fierce look on cold-rimmed face,
a bear's face in the cold flood,
you frisk and shiver like a fever
and then you heave away.
You strive with water, dark toadstool,
you look at it and snort;
it's as though you plough straight through
the foam of brittle waves;
you cut the salt sea open,
you must have the wave's heart.
Swift, lovely one, brave shadow,
skull of the sea, pillion to the strand,
a water-viper hoeing the wave,
with a look that frightens the heart.
White-bellied and good-natured
wanderer of the captive deep,
wild boar of the brine, in urgent mastery
he crosses the sea in a fine great sweep.
Throughout summer, when the weather changes,
he comes rocking along before the storm;
fierce boar, churn of hell-fury,
cross and greedy before the wild tide.
A spear with gold-crested breastplate,
a fish with a closed tunic;
sea's burden, two-breasted Leviathan,
he slips and catches along the wave's slope.
Saddle of the sea, take a bearing,
steer a course to the loud water,

dewis wryd, dos erof
yn gennad ŵr gwastad gof.
Dwg siwrnai o Fenai fwnc
dua Lysbwrn dilysbwnc,
a nofia yna ennyd
i fin Ysbaen, fynwes byd.
Nofiedydd o nef ydwyt;
nofia siás, gŵr nwyfys wyt.
Ymofyn ar derfyn dŵr,
mawr foliant, am ryfelwr,
Pirs Gruffudd, ond prudd pob bron,
perl iawngoel, pur lân galon,
parch y Penrhyn, impyn iach,
pôr addwyn, pwy ireiddiach?
Chwe blynedd, och o'i blined,
ar llong er pan aeth ar lled
i foroedd uwch y foryd,
dros y bar ar draws y byd.
Ond madws ydyw ymadael
â'r dŵr hallt yma i'r dewr hael,

i'w lys ei hun o le sâl;
ac aros man a garwn
a llawenhau'r holl llu hwn.
Ban welych ef, boen wiwlawn,
ar ei long yn wrol iawn,
galw arno, gloyw ei harnais,
galwad drwy gennad ar gais;
ac annerch ef, gynnyrch waith,
gwawd aml oddi wrth gydymaith
yn fwyn, gŵr a fu gynt
yn hwylio yr un helynt
nes iddo, hynaws addef,
brynu'i ddysg pan brinnodd ef.
A gwedi'n wir gwadu wnaeth
y môr a'i holl gymeriaeth.
Dod erthwch, dywed wrthaw,
dymuna droi'r damwain draw
a gado'r môr yn y man

choose a fathom, go on my behalf,
a messenger from a remembering man;
take your way from your bunk at Menai
unswervingly to Lisbon;
swim along there awhile
to the edge of Spain, heart of the world.
You are a heavenly swimmer,
swim to the chase, you lively one.
Ask at the water's limit
(let us give praise!) for a soldier,
Pirs Gruffudd, who saddened all breasts,
pearl of true faith, pure heart,
the honour of Penrhyn, its fine son,
gentle lord, lustiest of men.
It is six weary years
since he took ship abroad,
to the seas beyond the estuary,
over the bar across the world.
It's time for the gallant giver
to turn away from salt water
and come, ending anxiety,
to his own hall from that foul place,
to stay where I like to see him
and to please his people in this.
When, after this effort, you see him,
courageous upon his ship
in gleaming harness, call to him
a message on my behalf,
address him profitably
in copious verse from a companion
lovingly, from a man who once
sailed on the same journey
until, agreeable confession,
he bought knowledge as things went ill.
Then truly he forswore
the sea and all its ventures.
Now give a grunt and tell him,
beseech him to evade this fate
and soon to leave the sea

i rai eraill yr owran.
Anodd cael mael yn ael nos
ar y môr oer ymaros;
a drwg a gair anair yw
yn hawdd o'i ddilyn heddiw.
Da i ŵr ffraeth oddi ar draethell
dramwy'r byd a'r môr i bell
o ran cael, er oerni caeth,
yn y byd iawn wybodaeth;
a nid da gwn, na duwiol,
hir ddilyn hyn yn ei ôl.
Dangos, ffrom achos mewn ffrwyth,
diles galonau ei dylwyth.
O chwytha'r gwynt, chwith yw'r gwedd,
awel uchel ar lechwedd,
gwelir byd ynfyd anferth,
gweddio ac udo'n gerth
rhag ofn i'r gwynt, helynt dwys,
beryglu ei gorff briglwyd.
Llawer dyn llwyr adweinir
yn cwyno amdano i dir
heb gael huno, friwdro fron,
gwn fawr ddadl, gan freuddwydion.
Oferwyr ânt i foriaw
a gwŷr ni fedd droed fydd draw.
A doed ef, wedi dofi,
eto o'u mysg atom ni.
Doed adre, diwyd edrych,
i ledio'i wŷr i'w wlad wych.
Capten o Ras fel asur,
capten a'i bawen yn bur;
Duw o'i ras a ro'n drysor
ras iddo ymado â'r môr.

to others from now on.
There's little profit to be gained
waiting at dusk on the cold waters,
and much shame and evil comes
easily from sea-faring to-day.
It's good for a brisk man to leave the shore,
to sail the sea far over the world
to gain, though a cold captive,
true knowledge of this world.
But it's not good or godly
to keep on in this way.
Show his kin's unsatisfied hearts,
the fruit of a bitter cause.
When the wind blows and things look bad,
a high wind comes over the hillside,
the world goes mad and ugly,
there's praying and loud wailing
lest the wind, in this deep danger,
endanger his grey-headed body.
Many are then to be seen
groaning for his coming to land,
unable to sleep, in heart-break
and dreams; I've heard it much spoken of.
Wasters now go sea-faring,
men who own not a foot of land.
Let him be tamed to returning
from their company to ours.
Let him come home, devotedly
to lead his men to his fine land,
Captain of the azure *Grace*
and a clean-handed captain.
God in his grace will grant him
the treasure of giving up the sea.

46. Balet Cymraeg

ar fesur About the Bank of Helicon

Llef a roeson', llafar weision
doe a glywson' dan wŷdd gleision
        glwysaidd ac eglwysaidd;
tair oes i'r pencerddi tirion,
llinos o'r llwyn, eos wirion,
        dwysaidd baradwysaidd,
bronfraith bur araith berwalch,
mwyalch mwy ei awydd,
ysgydogyll drythyll dro
yn rhwydo llais yr hedydd,
        yn canu,
        yn tannu
        cymaint o awenydd;
        cyn hoywed,
        cyn groywed,
    ac yn gywir awydd.

Llwyn nid pell, nodau heb pallu,
llwyn Ebrillaidd llawn briallu,
        lle gwawd teg a llygaid tydd;
glyn a meillion Glanmai am allu
a gwyrdd ddillad gwir ddiwallu
        yn llenwi llawenydd;
a'r blodau ar drwynau'r drain,
a'r fedwen fain a'r glasddail;
gwiw yw'r ffynnon, glân yw'r man,
mae'n codi tan y gwiail
        y gloywddwr,
        y croy wddwr;
        lle teg llwyddiant,
        lle i gysgu,
        lle i ddysgu
    holl glymau o ddesgant.

46. A Welsh Ballad

upon the measure *About the Bank of Helicon*

A shout came from the loquacious ones
whom we heard yesterday under green trees,
　　holy and church-like place,
three lives to those gentle poets,
grove linnet, innocent nightingale,
　　pensive and paradisal,
sweet thrush of pure oration,
the blackbird greater in desire
and the lascivious siskin
who net the song of the lark,
　　singing,
　　plucking
　　so much poetry,
　　so lively,
　　so clearly,
and in their true lusting.

A near-by grove with notes increasing,
an April grove and primrose-full,
　　place of fine song and daisies;
a dale full of the spring clover
and the green clothes of true delight
　　filling with happiness,
with flowers on the thorn points,
the slim birch and the fresh leaves;
fair is the fountain, sweet the spot,
from under boughs there springs
　　the clear water,
　　the fresh water;
　　fair, fortunate place,
　　a place to sleep,
　　a place to learn
all knots of descanting.

Mynnwn bob mwynder i'm hannedd,
mynnwn ganu mwynen Gwynedd
    is gywir miwsig hoyw;
ar Wyddeles Eurwedd elwir,
ychen fannog crechwen feinir,
        mewn plas o goed glas gloyw,
canu yn llafar llawen hafau,
a'r adar yn gyfrodedd;
canu'n hylwydd gainc i'r Arglwydd,
eurgylch clod a mawredd;
        profiadau,
        caniadau,
        rhyw bynciau newidiog;
        dyfeisiau,
        tro lleisiau,
    llu oesoedd tra lluosog.

Aml yw cadair, amlwg coedydd,
aml yw colofn ddofn o ddeunydd,
        aml gwlwm mawl golau;
lle aml osteg llawn melystant
am ddigon mawl a ddygant
        deiliaid y dolau;
pob aderyn yn ei lais,
pob pren a'i bais yn laswyrdd,
pob llysieuyn yn ei rin,
pob edn a'i fin yn bencerdd,
        nid clwyfus
        ond nwyfus,
        rhyw bynciau nefol;
        nid tryblus
        ond treblus;
    Fenws piau'r faenol.

Da i ddynion eu diddanwch,
da i forwyn ei digrifwch,
        Duw Sul da i weision;
teg yw hyn, nid dig i henaint,
teg i ifainc, nid digofaint,

I'd have all sweetness in my house,
both the song of Gwynedd's darling
    to some sprightly music
and an Irish girl called Eurwedd,
unyoked pair of laughing girls
    in shining green tree mansion,
to sing loud of happy summers
all with bird song entwined;
profitably to sing to God
a golden cycle of great praise;
    a tuning up
    of psalmody
    in varying notes;
    devices,
    turning voices
  for unnumbered ages.

Many tree-clusters, open woodlands,
many a column deeply fashioned,
    many a clear knot of praise;
a peaceful place full of sweet chords
of the plentiful praise that's made
    by the meadow-dwellers;
each bird in its own voice,
each tree in bright green tunic,
each plant in its own virtue,
each bird with a poet's lips,
    not suffering
    but sprightly
    in heavenly notes;
    not troubled
    but in treble;
  the place is Venus's.

Delight is good for all mankind
and merriment for maidens,
    Sunday is good for men;
this is fair and not odious for age,
fair, not unpleasant, for youth.

Duw Sul da i weision;
teg y trefnodd gwir Dduw Dad
a'i rodd a'i rad mor hynod;
teg pob oslef, teg pob tro,
trwy na bo mo'r pechod.
Ar ddaear
mor glaear;
yn gynnar ar gwenith,
ar lwyndir;
mor fwyndir
lle y rhoddir y mawr fendith.

Sunday is good for men,
planned fair by the true God Father,
his gift and notable grace.
Each voice is fair, every turn,
as long as there's no sin.
On earth
how gentle;
early on the wheat
and on the grove;
how mild the land
where the great blessing's given!

47. Crys Y Mab

Fel yr oeddwn yn golchi
dan ben bont Aberteifi,
a golchffon aur yn fy llaw
a chrys fy nghariad i danaw,
fe ddaeth ataf ŵr ar farch
ysgwydd lydan, buan, balch,
ac a ofynnodd im a werthwn
crys y mab mwya' a garwn;
ac a ddwedais i na werthwn
er can punt nac er canpwn,
nac er llonaid y ddwy fron
o fyllt a defaid gwynion,
nac er llonaid dau gweirgae
o ychen dan eu hieuau,
nac er llonaid Llan Ddewi
o lysiau wedi sengi;
fel dyna modd y cadwn
crys y mab mwya' a garwn.

47. The Lover's Shirt

As I was washing under a span
of the bridge of Cardigan
and in my hand my lover's shirt
with a golden beetle to drub the dirt,
a man came to me on a steed,
broad in shoulder, proud in speed,
and he asked me if I'd sell
the shirt of the lad I love so well.

But I said I wouldn't sell
for a hundred pounds and packs as well,
nor if the grass of two ridges were deep
in wethers and the whitest sheep,
nor if two hay meadows were choked
with oxen which were ready yoked,
nor if St. David's nave were filled
with herbs all pressed but not distilled.
Not even for all that would I sell
the shirt of the lad I love so well.

Notes

1. Gododdin was the name of a tribe of North Britain living in what is to-day South East Scotland. Ptolemy the Geographer refers to them as Otadenoi. The name of the tribe was given to its heroic poem, *Gododdin.* Catraeth, as Sir Ifor Williams has shown, is the Catarracta or Cataractonium of the Romans, the Catterick of the English. Mynyddog Mwynfawr ruled from Dineiddyn or Dunedin. It is to be remembered that the Britons used horses in battle even before the Romans came and that they had learnt much about armour and fighting from the Romans. The English had neither horses nor such equipment. The odds of 300 trained commandos against thousands of the enemy are not incredible. Sir Ifor Williams dates this battle between 580-600, and this was when Aneirin lived and sang in Edinburgh.

    Mr. David Jones used the last line but one of the Issac stanza as the motto to his *In Parenthesis*, where this battle is related to the 1914–18 War.

2. Taliesin was another late sixth-century poet of North Britain, this time of Rheged, to-day the counties of Kirkcudbright, Wigtown and part of Ayr. He wrote in praise of Urien, King of Rheged, and his son Owain, both of whom fought against the Angles under Hussa, son of Ida. Hussa may be the Fflamddwyn or Flame-bearer of this poem.

    The text used is that of the *Book of Taliesin*, a manuscript of *c.* 1275.

3. Sir Ifor Williams has shown Heledd and Llywarch Hen to be not poets of the sixth or early seventh century but central figures in saga cycles composed in the ninth century. Pengwern is the modern Shrewsbury. Heledd, daughter of Cyndrwyn, here laments the death of her brother, Cynddylan, and the destruction of their home by the Mercians.

    The text used is that of *CLIH*.

4. Llywarch, in spite of doubts about him as a poet, was a historical person, a prince of North Britain during the sixth century. Hence the connection here with Urien Rheged.

    The text used is that of *CLIH*.

5. As Sir Ifor Williams says, only a similarity of style and the resulting accident of scribal assembling link this poem with Llywarch Hen and his saga. The sick man may have been a leper. I have here abstracted

the cuckoo sequence, the first ten *englynion* or thirty lines, from this poem.

The text used is that of *CLlH*.

6.   The names of some of these ancient British heroes are familiar to English readers in other forms. Cynfelyn is Cymbeline and his son Coel may be King Cole. Beli, the last of the heroes in the sequence, takes us back beyond history and legend to the Celtic gods. His name is remembered in Billingsgate.

Sir Ifor Williams believes this to be a collection of tail pieces originally belonging to the stories of the life and death of the people concerned. If this is so the stanzas have been not unskilfully strung together in *BBC* with an introductory opening and suitable conclusion, and with suitable questions occasionally to hold the interest. The sequence thus forms a complete poem, and one can imagine the poet or the narrator pausing, like a good entertainer, to ask his hearers in the hall for requests.

> Whose is this grave?
> It's so and so's grave;
> ask me, I know.

> *Piau y bedd hwn?*
> *Bedd hwn a hwn:*
> *gofyn i mi, mi a'i gwn.*

There are 72 of these fascinating stanzas in *BBC*, but no edited text of them has ever been published. I have translated others in *IWP*.

The text used here is that of *BBC*.

7.   This is the earliest and grimmest view we have of the Gereint of romance. Llongborth must have been a harbour in Southern England.

The text used is that of *BBC*.

8.   Meilyr Brydydd, or Meilyr the Poet, who lived during the early part of the twelfth century, was chief poet to Gruffudd ap Cynan, King of Gwynedd. Meilyr's son, Gwalchmai, and his grandsons were also poets. *Marwysgafn* meant deathbed, *ysgafn* being derived from the Latin *scamnum* (bench). Cynddelw and Bleddyn Fardd also wrote poems with the same title.

The text used here is that of *H*.

9.   Cynddelw Brydydd Mawr, or Cynddelw the Great Poet, who wrote during the second half of the twelfth century, was perhaps

the greatest master of his craft in that century. He wrote in praise
of princes of North and South Wales.

The text used here is that of *PG*.

10.   Gwalchmai, son of Meilyr, flourished during the middle of the
twelfth century, and sang in praise of Owain Gwynedd. His blending
of the themes of love, nature and war is similar to that effected by
Hywel ab Owain, whom he must have known well, but it is not
known which of the two poets first ventured upon this departure
from the conventions of bardism. Like Hywell, Gwalchmai described
the Battle of Tal y Moelfre and was probably present at it, for
Gwalchmai was a warrior as well as a poet. A landowner too, as the
place name Trewalchmai indicates.

The text used is that of *H*. 32 lines have been omitted where
lacunae make the text obscure. *V*. H., pp. 18–20.

11–18.   Hywel ab Owain Gwynedd was the son of the great Owain,
King of Gwynedd, and an Irish girl called Pyfog. He died in 1170
after a life of internecine and anti-Norman warfare. All his extant
verse is given here, and it is found in the *Hendregadredd MS*.

Caer Lliwelydd is the modern Carlisle; Kerry is in Montgomery-
shire; Maelienydd is a region of Central Wales; Rheged is South
Western Scotland; Tegeingl is the North Eastern corner of Wales.

Garwy Hir is one of the legendary great lovers of Britain. Ogrfan
is variously said to have been king of the underworld, father of
Guinevere and father of Ceridwen, who may have been a fertility
goddess and muse of poetry. Cynddelw, in his lament for the death
of Rhirid Flaidd, associates Ogrfan and Ceridwen. See Sir John Rhys,
Celtic Heathendom, pp. 267–9, for Ogrfan's cauldron and his connection with the alphabet. For the form Gogfran see p. 118. The battle
described is that of Tal y Moelfre, at which Hywel fought at his
father's side against Henry II's army and fleet, the latter reinforced
by foreign contingents. Gwalchmai also describes this battle.

19.   Gruffudd ab yr Ynad Coch belongs to the second half of the
thirteenth century. This great poem is the only one attributed to him
with certainty. Llywelyn ap Gruffudd was the last independent ruler
of Wales and this poem expresses a suitable and unusual feeling of
awful tragedy and national disaster. It is something of a *tour de force*
in that it has only one main end rhyme throughout its considerable
length.

The translator is faced with difficulties such as the ambiguity in the use of the word *penn* which cannot be rendered by one word in English. *Penn milwr*, for instance, means both a soldier's head and a soldier-leader. The text used is that of *PRBH*.

20. Gruffudd ab Adda was a poet and a musician as well as the author of two famous essays in poetic prose (see *Yr Areithiau Pros*, D. Gwenallt Jones. Welsh Univ. Press 1934). He was a contemporary of Dafydd ap Gwilym, who lamented his death in verse. The pacification of Welsh life in the fourteenth century is well reflected in this poem, but Gruffudd ab Adda himself died in a friendly scuffle.
The text used is that of *CDGG*.

21–23. The dates of Dafydd ap Gwilym's life are not known, but he flourished during the middle decades of the fourteenth century. He was born at Llanbadarn in Cardiganshire and was buried at Strata Florida Abbey. The idea has now been abandoned that Morfudd and Dyddgu were just any fair or dark-haired girl respectively, with whom Dafydd was for the moment in love, and Dr. Thomas Parry has established the case for their having been real women. Dafydd wrote about thirty poems to Morfudd, and the poems show her to have been blonde, of noble birth, married, a native of Northern Cardiganshire and not unwilling to continue to receive the poet to the arms he celebrated in a *cywydd*. Of Morfudd's husband Dafydd made the type of a jealous cuckold, who became a stock character in poetry for more than two hundred years after.
In *The Woodland Mass* Dafydd employs the wandering scholar's trick of using religious terminology to speak of nature and love-making, but it is possible to recognise an awareness of the ubiquity of the glory of God here rather than blasphemy.
The Rattle Bag is a fine example of the vituperative, rabelaisian mode much affected by fourteenth-century poets, especially Dafydd's often unprintable contemporaries Madog Dwygraig and Dafydd y Coed. The heaping together of compound descriptive words, such as we see in the line: *greithgrest garegddwyn grothgro*, was one of the skills of the mediaeval Welsh craftsman in words, and Dafydd was our greatest master of it.
The text used here is that of *GDG*.

24. Llywelyn Goch ap Meurig Hen wrote during the second half of

the fourteenth century. Most of his verse is in the traditional range of praise to patrons in the *awdl* form, but in this *cywydd* he does something staggeringly new in singing an aubade to a dead girl, who sleeps too long in her dark earth-bed.

The text is that of *CDGG*.

25–6. Iolo Goch, a master poet of wide learning and scope in subject matter, flourished during the second half of the fourteenth century. He wrote in praise of Owain Glyndŵr and his hall at Sycharth. No one appreciated comfort, food and drink, and the respect due to a master poet more than Iolo, or expressed this better in verse.

Hu Gadarn, or Hugh the Strong, is the Hugue li Forz of the twelfth century French metrical *Pélerinage de Charlemagne*, which was translated into Welsh in the fourteenth century. A Welsh text is included in the *Red Book of Hergest* and this was translated into English by Sir John Rhys for Koschwitz's treatise on the French poem (*Heilbronn* 1879). The description of a fourteenth-century plough is detailed and exact.

The text of Iolo Goch is from *CIGE*.

27. Siôn Cent (Anglicé John Kent, for Siôn is pronounced Shone) wrote during the early decades of the fifteenth century. It is not easy to distinguish his identity, except as a poet, from that of other John Kents, John Kemps and John a Kents of the fifteenth century. He recommended the remembrance of death to the proud and wealthy ones of this world and was the first poet to be consistently unflattering in his reference to the landed aristocracy.

The sectional form of this *cywydd*, with its refrain, is unusual in Welsh.

The text is that of *CIGE*.

28–31. Dafydd ab Edmwnd, who flourished during the second half of the fifteenth century, was a poet of love and nature in the tradition of Dafydd ap Gwilym. A great craftsman in verse, he was responsible for the tightening up of the twenty-four strict measures of versification at the Carmarthen Eisteddfod of 1451. Living at a time when many poets were involved in the Wars of the Roses, Dafydd ab Edmwnd avoided politics, but his attitude towards England is made clear in his lament for his dead friend Siôn Eos, the harpist.

In the poem concealing the identity of his love it is interesting to see Welsh forms of Norman-French girls' names Sioned, Annes,

Alswn, Alis and Isabel take their place alongside the accustomed Gwenhwyfar, Gwenllian and Nest.

Siôn Eos would be John Nightingale in English.

The text of the Dafydd ab Edmwnd poems is based on *GDE*, except that of the poem *I Wallt Merch*, which is from *YFN*.

32.   Bedo Aeddren or Aurdrem flourished about the year 1500. His work is confused in the manuscripts with that of Bedo Brwynlys and some of his verse, including this poem, has been attributed to Dafydd ap Gwilym. This Easter poem is clearly in the Dafydd ap Gwilym tradition and has rare freshness and light. It was printed as Dafydd's work in *BDG* but is rejected by Sir Ifor Williams and Dr. Thomas Parry.

The text here used is that of *MS Llanstephan* 133 *p.* 1066.

33.   Lewis Glyn Cothi took his name from the Cothi valley in Northern Carmarthenshire, where he was born. He took the Lancastrian side in the Wars of the Roses and got into trouble for it. He lived during the middle and second half of the fifteenth century.

Saint Dwynwen was the daughter of the fifth-century Brychan Brycheiniog and the patroness of lovers.

Lewis Glyn Cothi's work is in process of being edited by Mr. E. D. Jones and one volume has appeared. The text here used is based on the early sixteenth century *MS Llanstephan* 7, where the poem is headed 'Marwnat John y Glynn mab v mlwydd Lewis y Glynn i Dat ai Kant', 'Lament for the death of John of the Valley, five years old son of Lewis of the Valley, sung by his father'.

34.   Tudur Aled, a native of Llansannan in Denbighshire, flourished 1480–1526. Like Dafydd ap Gwilym and Dafydd ab Edmwnd, he was of noble stock. He was a strict upholder of tradition in poetry and an appreciater of good fare. No Welsh poet has written in more lively fashion or with keener observation of animals. The poem of asking became a conventional type, affording the poet the opportunity to exercise his ingenuity in the invention of comparisons.

The text here is that of *YFN*.

35–6.   The text of these *englynion* is based on that of *MS Mostyn* 131, (pp. 132 and 440), a collection of *englynion* by many authors in the hand of John Jones, Gelli Lyfdy, written between 1605 and 1618.

37.   This is a selection from an *englyn* sequence of considerable charm.

T. Gwynn Jones copied some of them for his *Gelfyddyd Gwta*, printed them as separate *englynion* and altered them.

The text is based on that of *MS Mostyn* 131 (p. 9).

38. It was William Thomas's chaplain, Syr Siôn Gruffudd, who wrote the well-known *Hiraeth am Gaernarfon*, when they were together in Flanders *c.* 1586.

The text is based on that of *MS Mostyn* 131 (p. 311).

39. Robin Clidro, a native of the Clwyd valley, was a wandering poet of the *clerwr* or lower class who lived during the second half of the sixteenth century. An elegy by Siôn Tudur tells us that he was killed by a highwayman in South Wales. His poetry is lively and amusing and he used verse form and *cynghanedd* with a cheerfully unbardic freedom for which one is thankful.

The text used here is that of *MS Cwrt Mawr* 24, a manuscript of the seventeenth century. An incomplete copy of this poem was printed by T. Gwynn Jones in his *Llên Cymru* Vol. III.

40. The Cynon River is a tributary of the Taff. The text used is that of *CRhC*.

Rowenna, daughter of Hengist, was given the name Alis Ronwen in a Triad. The English kings decended from her marriage with Vortigern were called Alice's children by the Welsh.

41. This is the second scene of the five-act tragedy. In the main the unknown author depends on Chaucer and Henryson, selecting freely and translating closely from them. But there is no known source for this version of Cressida's trial, which may therefore be taken to be original writing. The author was a scholar who found no difficulty in reading Chaucer and Henryson. He must have formed his notion of dramatic structure and tragic irony in the Elizabethan London theatre. His tragedy, though not as great or as original as Shakespeare's *Troilus and Cressida*, gives an entirely different presentation of the story and has more unity.

Mr. Herbert Davies's production of my prepared text of *Troelus a Chresyd* at the Ystradgynlais National Eisteddfod of 1954 (the first known performance) showed that this unique Welsh tragedy can hold the theatre.

The text is from *MS Peniarth* 106, the sole version, which was written by John Jones, Gelli Lyfdy. About half of it was completed by February 1613 and the rest by the autumn of 1622. It is clearly a copy. The play must have been written *c*. 1600.

42.   William Cynwal wrote this poem to defend women against the attack upon them written in a Skeltonic metre by an unknown poet earlier in the sixteenth century, a poem which I translated in *The Rent that's Due to Love*, Poetry London, 1950 and more fully in *Against Women*, Golden Cockerel Press, 1953. Cynwal, who died in 1587 or 1588, took one of his poetic grades at the Caerwys Eisteddfod of 1568. He was a strict observer of the bardic traditions, but here he descends to a stanza form of the free metres, such as an unqualified poet of the lowest order might have used, since the subject matter of this poem is outside the conventional range of the master poet.

The text used is that of *CRhC*.

43-5.   Thomas Prys, of Plas Iolyn, Denbighshire, was a landowner, a soldier, a pirate and a good poet. The dates of his life are *c*. 1564–1634. He was at Tilbury with the Queen in 1588 and fought in the Low Countries, probably with Sir Roger Williams. He knew London well, its great houses, taverns, brothels and prisons, and has some amusing and some bitter things to say about it. More than 200 of his *cywyddau* have come down to us and they are all worth reading. No poet in Welsh has as wide a scope of subject or writes in a more lively way. Nor was he deficient in the traditional skill of versification in the strict metres.

The text used here is that of *MS Mostyn* 112, which may be in the poet's hand, with occasional readings from the Cefn Coch MSS. I have left the Welsh original of the sea-battle poem untouched, for to attempt modernisation of spelling would destroy the interest of the English phrases woven into the metrical form, phrases which may be picked out in their Welsh spelling.

A note in the margin of this manuscript informs us that *Grace* was the name of Pirs Gruffudd's ship. Pirs, to whom Prys sends the porpoise as a messenger, was Prys's cousin and heir to the Penrhyn estate, but he was not wise enough to give up buccaneering, as Prys did, and he got into more and more trouble. Pirs Gruffudd died in 1628 and was buried in Westminster Abbey.

46.   Edmwnd Prys, Archdeacon of Merioneth, lived from 1544–1623. He helped in the translation of the Bible into Welsh and versified the Psalms. He wrote both in the free and strict metres. He carried on a long controversy in verse with William Cynwal, who considered him

no poet at all, so prepared was he to use popular and even foreign stanza forms, as in this Welsh Ballad.

The text is from *CRhC.*

47.   The text of this song is from *CRhC.*

For the poems of the fourteenth, fifteenth and sixteenth centuries I have used different edited versions and manuscripts. I plead this in excuse for inconsistencies which may appear in the presentation of the Welsh text.

Abbreviations

<table>
<tr><td>BBC:</td><td>The Black Book of Carmarthen: Reproduced by J. G. Evans, Pwllheli, 1907.</td></tr>
<tr><td>BDG:</td><td>Barddoniaeth Dafydd ap Gwilym: William Owen and Owen Jones, London, 1789.</td></tr>
<tr><td>CA:</td><td>Canu Aneirin: Ifor Williams, Cardiff, 1938.</td></tr>
<tr><td>CDGG:</td><td>Cywyddau Dafydd ap Gwilym a'i Gyfoeswyr: T. Roberts and Ifor Williams, Bangor, 1914. (2nd ed. Cardiff, 1935.)</td></tr>
<tr><td>CIGE:</td><td>Cywyddau Iolo Goch ac Eraill: Henry Lewis, Thomas Roberts and Ifor Williams, Cardiff, 1937.</td></tr>
<tr><td>CLlH:</td><td>Canu Llywarch Hen: Ifor Williams, Cardiff, 1935.</td></tr>
<tr><td>CRhC:</td><td>Canu Rhydd Cynnar: T. H. Parry-Williams, Cardiff, 1932.</td></tr>
<tr><td>GDE:</td><td>Gwaith Dafydd ab Edmwnd: T. Roberts, Bangor, 1914.</td></tr>
<tr><td>GDG:</td><td>Gwaith Dafydd ap Gwilym: T. Parry, Cardiff, 1952.</td></tr>
<tr><td>H:</td><td>The Hendregadredd Manuscript: Rh. Morris Jones, J. Morris Jones and T. H. Parry-Williams, Cardiff, 1953.</td></tr>
<tr><td>IWP:</td><td>An Introduction to Welsh Poetry: Gwyn Williams, London, 1953.</td></tr>
<tr><td>PG:</td><td>The Poetry of the Gogynfeirdd: E. Anwyl, Denbigh, 1909.</td></tr>
<tr><td>PRBH:</td><td>Poetry from the Red Book of Hergest: J. G. Evans, Pwllheli, 1911.</td></tr>
<tr><td>YFN:</td><td>Y Flodeugerdd Newydd: W. J. Gruffydd, Cardiff, 1909.</td></tr>
</table>

Index